W9-BES-808

Caring: A Daughter's Story

CARING
A DAUGHTER'S STORY
Diane Rubin

Holt, Rinehart and Winston
New York

Published by Holt, Rinehart and Winston,
383 Madison Avenue, New York, New York 10017.

Published simultaneously in Canada by Holt, Rinehart
and Winston of Canada, Limited.

Library of Congress Cataloging in Publication Data
Rubin, Diane.
Caring

1. Breast—Cancer—Patients—United States—Biography.
2. Cerebrovascular disease—Patients—United States—Biography.
3. Parents, Aged—United States—Family relationships.
4. Parents, Aged—Health and hygiene. 5. Rubin, Mildred.
6. Rubin, Seybert. I. Title.
RC280.B8R8   362.1′4′0922   81-6987   AACR2
ISBN Hardbound: 0-03-058938-X

FIRST EDITION
Printed in the United States of America
10 9 8 7 6 5 4 3 2 1

ISBN 0-03-058938-X

To Joel

"An ancient grandmother lived with her daughter and her grandson in a small but comfortable house not far from the village. The old woman grew frail and feeble, her eyesight became dimmer every day, and she found it hard to remember where she'd put things and what people had asked her to do. Instead of being a help around the house she became a constant trial and irritation. She broke the plates and cups, lost the knives, put out the stove, and spilled the water. One day, exasperated because the older woman had broken another precious plate, the younger one gave some money to her son and told him, 'Go to the village and buy your grandmother a wooden plate. At least we will have one thing in the house she cannot break.'

"The boy hesitated because he knew that wooden plates were used only by peasants and servants—not by fine ladies like his grandmother—but his mother insisted, so off he went. Some time later he returned bringing not one, but two, wooden plates.

" 'I only asked you to buy one,' his mother said to him sharply. 'Didn't you listen to me?'

" 'Yes,' said the boy. 'But I bought the second one so there will be one for you when you get old.' "

—A PAKISTANI FOLK TALE
from *You and Your Aging Parent*
by Barbara Silverstone and
Helen Kandel Hyman

"One recent study has indicated that it is not marriage, parenthood, grandparenthood, the climacteric, or the empty nest, but the responsibility of caring for aging parents that is becoming *the* major problem in the family and a primary source of life stress."

—BERNICE NEUGARTEN,
Professor of Human Development,
University of Chicago

Acknowledgments

I am in debt to many people.

Phyllis Allyne, Anne Quinn, Abe Dorn, Geraldine Spain, and Leonard Abrams smoothed a lot of rough spots in the past three difficult years. So did the busy staff in Roger Daniels's office. Marilyn Bertram, Lois Carr, Resa Cherry, Terry Dezzi, Sherry Estren, Dorothy Gorbeck, Barbara Graef, Gina Hopman, Sandy Kaltz, Binnie Kaplan, Brucie Kaufman, Karen Lauenschild, Jeanne Piannelli, Kay Thomas, and Beth Viner were unfailingly compassionate and kind.

JoAnn Downes, Ginette Ferzst, and Al Gardner—members of the Hospice team at Pennsylvania Hospital—comforted my mother faithfully. Jeffrey Hartzell, medical director of the Hospice, did several kindnesses for me.

I thank David Cook, neurologist, who gave much more than his extraordinary medical skill to Mother. He gave her hope. He gave her time. He was her friend.

I thank lovely, loving Miriam Shore, both for emotional

support and for the family strengths she brought to light.

I feel gratitude, respect, and much affection toward Roger Daniels for his kindness and compassion, his skill, his time, his endless efforts on behalf of Mother, his amazing and contagious optimism, his honesty.

Finally, for all of the above—and for their love—I thank my family and friends.

Eight years ago Dan Rottenberg urged me to begin to write. I thank him for his confidence as well as his continued interest in my work. My thanks to Judy Grossman for her early and ongoing help with this manuscript; her corrections and suggestions and support were invaluable. Jennifer Josephy, my editor, has taught me much. I am grateful for her guidance, judgment, and encouragement.

Caring: A Daughter's Story

Introduction

On September 18, 1978, at 11:15 A.M., my mother started chemotherapy. At 12:05 that night my father had a stroke. By the middle of the following day, I—a busy, healthy, not exceptionally unselfish forty-two-year-old woman—had become my parents' primary caretaker.

This is the story of that experience.

Taking care of ailing parents was no novelty for me. My mother's health had always been a problem; my father's, in the previous ten years, had gradually declined. I'd dosed and bathed, dressed and fed, massaged, ice-packed, and heating-padded them many times, but always with the certainty that they would shortly mend and I would soon return to normal life.

My normal life, when the September crisis hit, consisted of the average mix of problems for someone my age: a child's acne, midlife pains, periodic marital friction, doubts about commitments, decisions, the future, my judgment, and myself. But it also held some blessings: a twenty-two-year marriage to Joel, a fifty-one-year-old business executive, and our two sons—Bill, a college junior, age twenty, and Rich, a seventeen-year-old junior in high school. Both boys, by then, looked like survivors of my second worst ordeal up to that time: their adolescences. There were other plusses, too. Our health was reasonably good. We frequently agreed on what was funny. We weren't rich, but we were comfortable.

My nearly empty nest did not loom threateningly that fall. I had begun to write four years before, had several pieces published, and was starting to receive notes from editors asking to see more of my work. My most recent piece entitled "Fear of Climbing," recounting my *worst* ordeal—twelve days in the desert on an Outward Bound adult women's course—appeared in *Philadelphia* magazine in April 1978, and was scheduled to be condensed in the October issue of *Reader's Digest.* I was having splendid luck for a beginner and was starting to gain confidence in my ability to write. "The Aging Parent Problem" was on my list of possible future topics.

The Aging Parent Problem: Words that marked a folder growing fat with articles on nursing homes and pieces about parent abuse. Where I filed grisly clippings on matricide, the crime a child rarely tried to hide but always felt compelled to justify by saying, "I couldn't stand to see my mother suffer anymore."

The Aging Parent Problem: A label for what many of my friends were struggling with. A subject that I could cluck about compassionately. A pigeonhole for *other* people's pain.

And then *my* parents faltered. The questions other caring children wrestled with—life and death and limits on one's time; love and money, hate and rage, resentment and compassion and fatigue—seemed to belong exclusively to me every moment of my waking day and in my dreams. I was terrified and overwhelmed by the likelihood that this time there would not be any out for me until somebody died.

My journal entries turned into long diatribes about my parents' pain, my parents' needs, my rising panic. I cursed the gods in every entry. Cursed the universe. I cursed myself. I screamed and whined page after angry page, hoping that the words would soothe the hurt.

When I finally stopped complaining long enough to see beneath the misery, some tiny truths emerged: my Outward Bound trip, for example, when compared to full-time caring for sick parents, loomed in memory about as taxing as a sunbath. What I was howling about every day became my All-Time Worst Ordeal. I grew more aware daily that if it was so hard for me, who had so much, it must have been an utter hell for children who were poorer. Or those much more alone. I wondered whether anyone could do a decent job of caring for sick parents.

The Aging Parent Problem was suddenly concrete and my vantage point firsthand.

It was then that I decided I would write about my struggle. Not only to impose some order on what felt like total chaos, but to search for sense in such adversity.

I knew, from the beginning, *that* would have to be my theme. I didn't have to take a giant step to put myself in either parent's place. Who *couldn't* imagine the hell of going through each day exquisitely aware of having cancer? I didn't have to be an Actors' Studio graduate to fantasize the fears my father must have felt: Would the next stroke leave him paralyzed? Could he *survive* another stroke? And if he didn't, what would happen to my mother?

But as much as I could empathize, and as deep as I believed my understanding was, I also knew my insights were no more than secondhand. As much as I might *think* I hurt for them, my *parents* were the ones who really bled.

I therefore wouldn't dare to set down their experience. To

ask them to reveal their feelings and fears would add to their already overflowing cup of trouble. To guess would be to trivialize their pain.

My struggle—only what *I* knew about for certain—would have to be the theme.

In November I informed my parents and my sister that I planned to write a book about what taking care was like for *me*. They agreed that many of my problems were most likely what many others in my place were feeling too. They thought my words might comfort by reminding other people that they were not unique.

They gave me their okay.

They read the book in progress, and while they were not always overjoyed with everything I felt, they never gave me less than their encouragement. And, except for saying that they wished I hadn't told their ages, they never hinted that I ought to change a word.

Experts claim the problem of parental caretaking is serious and growing. They blame it on changes in the family structure, increased mobility, and a medical technology that prolongs the life span. But, beyond extending sympathy and giving tips on picking nursing homes and telling what plan B of Medicare will cover, experts rarely say the things you really need to know.

I am not an expert, but three years of slogging through have taught me this: ethical abstractions—"shoulds" and "oughts" and "obligations"—do not have a thing to do with day-to-day caring. Taking decent care of ailing parents has to do with learning to endure a universe of feelings, withstanding endless guilt, and simply muddling through. Above all, it has to do with trying to do good and simultaneously fighting to stay sane.

May 3–September 18

"Would you ask again?" my father said.

It was 8:15. We'd been waiting an hour and a half.

I checked for the third time. "She's next," I said. "The secretary told me that they're running late, but she's definitely next."

Mother scraped the paper slippers, lit her seventh cigarette, and clutched the wrinkled cotton hospital gown. She looked around the waiting room. "Maybe you should change the bone scan time," she said to me too loudly. "If they don't take me soon I'll never make it there by ten o'clock. I wouldn't want to keep someone else from using that appointment."

My father flipped the pages of a magazine. He tapped his feet impatiently and shifted in the sculptured plastic seat he was too fat for. The ashes from his cigarette fell on the floor.

I made notes and sipped tea. I checked to see that my sister's number and a dime were handy so I could call her when we learned the verdict. Not that there was any doubt. But I had told her that I would call her as soon as we heard.

"Mildred Rubin, please."

A surgical nurse—looking harassed so early in the day—appeared at the door and shouted out my mother's name: "Mildred Rubin."

Mother stood and quickly summoned up her courage; the shoulders back, the straightened spine, the chin thrust out defiantly, the tiny frosted head held high. She marched away to surgery. Again.

She was perpetually ill. The darkened bedroom air was always gray and sickly sour. Newspapers lay where they had fallen on the floor. A wormy brown extension cord connected the blue heating pad to the place where her body hurt.

She was such a sickly child—"always whining, always feeling bad"—that her puzzled mother took her to a "yiddel" for opinions. This ghetto-dwelling scholar of the yolk—a little bearded man with dirty hands—would roll an egg around her skull, break it open in a bowl, and analyze its shape before he'd make a diagnosis.

He didn't help.

But legitimate practitioners did little better. Throughout her adult life my mother progressed from pain through misery to agony and back. She had a pregnancy from which she nearly died that had to be aborted. She suffered from nausea, migraines, arthritis, and colitis all her life. She underwent two operations on her ovaries, later a hysterectomy, and five operations on her spine, including fusions and removal of degenerated discs. In 1974, at sixty-two, she had a mastectomy. In late January 1978, there was a lump in her groin which proved to be a spread of tumor. This May . . . today . . . another lump.

We wait to find out what it signifies.

My mother's recurrent catastrophic illness turned my fa-

6

ther, Seybert, seventy-one, into my healthy parent. He had survived two major strokes, a massive heart attack, and scores of ischemic episodes that warned of insufficient blood supplies to narrowed arteries. Although his list of symptoms read like *The Merck Manual*—a chronic case of gout, intermittent numbness in the toes, prostate problems, lower back pain, cataracts, angina—he was—compared with mother—in the pink.

In ways other than their health, my parents deviated from the model parent mean. My pretty, sleek, sweetly perfumed mother was never plump and flour-dusted. She didn't fix me milk and cookies; she never joined the PTA. If she weren't writhing in her bed or scrubbing floors, she'd be tracking down her bookie for the point spread on the Phillies or the Eagles or the A's. If her body wasn't racked with pain and if the house was spotless, she'd be running off to bingo games or poker or canasta. She didn't like to cook, wouldn't even read a recipe. "I can't. They're too confusing." But every night she studied racing forms—pored through pedigrees and weights and past performances to pick tomorrow's winner.

My handsome father's coat of arms could have been two dice above a flashing neon sign: EVERYTHING IN EXCESS. He was an overdoer, a man who wanted more. Throughout his married life he had fought with Mother over money, fidelity, excessive generosity to friends, acquaintances, and, not infrequently, strangers. His life was overrun with bets—good, bad, sure, and side—and heavy, endless debts.

My sister, Alice, thirty-seven, had little tolerance for sham, a short attention span, and an even shorter fuse. Her inner wiring ran direct from heart to mouth, which meant that half her life was spent regretting ill-timed statements and the other half accepting grateful thanks for hundreds of impulsive, loving acts. She was single and my father helped support her, which caused friction. More sparks flew as my mother told her what to wear, or how to speak, or what to do each time they were together. She and I had little contact, but when we did, we hissed like crossed wires. Her health was up to family par: she had diabetes.

They were the wrong family for me. I always felt I should have been related to brilliant, wealthy, witty folk instead of two good-looking bettors and a pudgy stick of TNT. True, they had some qualities I liked: their way of keeping sane by maintaining a sense of humor; their generosity. But I hated Mother's habits, Daddy's emotional distance, my sister's unpredictability. I wished, and tried, to live as if I'd fallen miles from my gnarled family tree.

Which is not to say I didn't love them. They were family, after all, and we were Jews, which meant I was connected to an old and strong tradition of commitment to the genealogical line. And though I might have wished I wasn't *theirs,* I always knew they were, irrevocably, mine.

Still punchy from the Pentothal, Mother stumbled toward the dressing room and said, "I have to hurry. They said I have to get injected with a dye."

Her smell was concentrated in the tiny room: a mix of medicine and musk, Shalimar and surgery. I knew it very well.

I held the navy slacks for her to step into. I slipped the blue and white silk blouse around her back. "You button, while I try to find a wheelchair," I directed.

"No. I'm walking," Mother said.

"The surgeon said it is another spread," my father told us as we walked to Nuclear Medicine.

"I'm not surprised," said Mother, shrugging.

Nor I. But just the same . . . I shivered.

She found the lump in her right breast in 1974.

"What are you going to do?" I asked when she told me she had to see a surgeon at four-thirty that day.

"Whatever he tells me to," she said.

"Like hell," I yelled into the phone.

"Whatever he tells me to . . ."

My mother's lifelong litany. She would have handed her sick body over, without question, to *anyone* in white in the hope that being "good" would make her better. If somebody prefixed "doctor" said her liver should come out, she would have shrugged and blinked her eyes and sighed and signed the form as long as she was guaranteed a private room.

I couldn't leave it up to her.

Daddy was befogged from his first stroke, and Alice was in her customary spin.

I had to find out what the options were. I had to figure out what she should do.

Dr. Crile's book convinced me that the Halstead Radical was statistically no better than a modified mastectomy. All I had to do was find a local surgeon who'd concur. Not a simple matter then. For three sweaty days in May 1974 I dragged my mother in and out of seven consultations. In the end, two specialists agreed with me and Dr. Crile.

"*You* must choose," I said to Mother, persisting in the sham that she was capable of making an informed choice.

She opted for the modified.

But the cancer spread.

It haunted me. What if I had minded my own business?

"I won't take chemotherapy," she said throughout the month of May. "That's final."

Mother's words, I knew, were unrelated to what she finally would do. But she said, at least four times a week, "It's bad enough I'm deformed. I won't be bald. I won't take chemotherapy. That's definite."

Mother's doctor—Roger Daniels—asked to meet with us on June 5. "By then, I'll have assessed the scans, gotten the results of tissue tests, and consulted with the oncologist," he said.

9

Mother thought he was a saint. "He's so polite," she said.

He was a slender, graying man, somewhere in his middle forties, impeccably dressed, pressed, and mannered.

"I've never known anyone so kind," she said.

I'd never known anyone so quick. It seemed to me his specialty was less internal medicine than medicine done faster than the speed of sound, or medicine attempted under stress. He was always running late or wanted on the intercom or on the telephone. Or in another room for "just a moment." Although he seemed to be serene, I doubted anyone so swift would not be superficial.

We wait in his office. The carpet is tan. A single painting, beige and bland, is hanging on the flaxen-colored walls. My parents sit on leather chairs before a tidy desk of cherry wood; I'm on a bench. Alice isn't here. I have to call her when we're done.

The doctor is late. Mother hums and does a crossword puzzle. Daddy fidgets. I take notes.

"Hi folks." The doctor slides into his seat. "The nodule in your groin was cancerous again," he says. "But we expected that and that's not so important. What does concern me, Mildred, is that the cancer has spread up to your neck. But even that's not *dire*. Your estrogen receptors tested positive, which means the tumor is likely to respond to a new drug I'm going to prescribe. Tomaxafin. A hormone."

Mother tries to look alert. She shakes her head as if she understands, but I know she hasn't heard a thing. She is waiting for the word on chemotherapy.

"However, I'm afraid there's news that's not so good," the doctor says.

Her skinny shoulders stiffen.

"The oncologist says you should have radiation on your neck. It will relieve the pain and it should stop additional spread."

"You mean I don't need chemotherapy?"

"That's right. Now any questions?"

10

She runs behind the desk. She's hugging him. "Oh, thank you, Dr. Daniels. Thank you very much."

He smiles politely, tries to hide his puzzled look, then proceeds. "As for side effects, you might have dryness of the mouth, some loss of hair in back of neck, perhaps some nausea, and some problems swallowing. . . ."

His voice trails off. He stops at last, aware he might as well inform a flagpole of the side effects of thunderstorms.

"Thank you, Dr. Daniels."

She's like a child whose bedtime's been postponed for a half hour.

"Thank you. Thanks a lot."

My mother, having been informed the cancer's traveled to her bones, prescribed a powerful hormone, ordered to take cobalt treatments for twenty-one consecutive days, responds by *thanking* her doctor. Over and over. A million times.

"*Grazia*," she says. "*Merci*."

I couldn't stand to see it.

If Mother wasn't acting like exiled Russian royalty, she played the pathetic peasant begging her master not to beat her for offenses such as bumping into walls.

Arrogant sometimes. Sometimes apologetic. And always, with a doctor, groveling.

"Tell me again about the hormones, please."

It is clear to me *today* that Alice's attempt to understand was rational and my response was rotten and insane. At the time, however, Alice asked me after I had spent the morning driving, picking up and dropping off our parents, looking for a parking place. After I had waited, witnessed Mother's maddening response to Dr. Daniels, gone back to get the car, and found a twenty-five-dollar ticket on the window of my station wagon. After I had picked up my parents again and re-deposited them at their apartment just before racing back to my home to try to do my own day's work with less than half a day remaining.

Alice had been sitting in her office.

11

"What do hormones have to do with stemming Mother's spread?" she asked.

As if the Nobel Prize depended on my answer, I regurgitated everything about ovaries I'd heard; my busy mouth brimmed with polysyllables; I wove a tapestry entwining threads of estrogen with every variation on adrenal emanations I could think of.

Alice was not impressed.

"Talk right," she said. "And don't pontificate to me."

"Drop dead," I said, slipping quickly from my role as Madame Curie and back into my big sister act.

During the summer of 1978 my mother showed a side of herself that I had seen only once before. In 1972, when the operations on her spine, some fourteen acupuncture treatments, and ten sessions with a hypnotist had failed to end her misery, she checked into a pain clinic in La Crosse, Wisconsin, where, I swear, she received a backbone transplant.

Letters from someone who *signed* herself my mother started coming twice a week. Letters full of hope and full of health.

"Dr. Shealy says I am an inspiration to the patients," Mother wrote. Supposedly.

"I'm feeling good and getting stronger by the day."

I was sure she had hired a ghostwriter.

But no amanuensis did the yoga stretches she so proudly showed me on her first day home. Nor did another mother say that it was time to fire her maid because "the housework keeps me moving and I need the exercise." And no one forged the letter that the doctor wrote to Mother's sister Ethel in December of that year, thanking her for thanking him for helping mother:

"It really makes me most happy to know that Milly has reached home in her improved state, and I join with you in praying that it will last. She was a great delight to have here, and we miss the inspiration which she conveyed to the other patients. Give her my love and tell her I will paddle her behind if she doesn't keep it up!"

Mother joined the Y. Every day, before her lunch date with "the girls," she would plunge into a public pool and swim five laps. Rest and naps were stricken from her schedule. "I don't lie down," she would say, "unless it's time to sleep."

She was remade, and she stayed brand-new until my father had his stroke. Then—was it inevitable?—worry and the need to nurse him flattened all her good intentions. Things unraveled, quickly.

But in the summer of her radiation Mother was inspired again.

Shrugging off the muggy heat and frequent rains of Philadelphia summers, she waited every day without complaint for a bus to take her back and forth to X-ray.

"I'll be glad to drive you, Mom," I said, praying she would refuse.

"Thanks. But no. I need to do it by myself."

The radiation browned her face and neck, but she didn't whine. She laughed when people praised her lovely suntan. Her mouth was sore; food needed to be mush. She chewed behind a napkin, not wanting to offend, and thanked the Lord that she could eat at all.

She was nothing like the mother I had known. I was confused.

Midlife took on new meaning that long summer. Instead of being rich with possibility—the way the best sellers assured me it would be when I entered my middle forties—it felt profoundly sad.

Many of my friends were facing problems with their parents: Shirley's mother went into a mental hospital in May. Mort found a nursing home for his unconscious father that appeased his conscience, but didn't fit his pocketbook. He

13

would have to take the money he had saved for his children's college education and spend it on his dad. *Later* he would borrow for tuition. Susan had to pay her parents' rent. Uncle Ben was hospitalized for kidney tests. Barry's father, on his daily walk, got lost two times in June and seven times in July. Debbie and Ina mourned their father's sudden death.

Everybody's parents seemed to be upon the brink of something dire. Midlife felt more like a precipice than a threshold.

My friends and I were scared and unprepared. To toilet train our children we had read the experts and been able to relax. We'd gotten ready in advance for empty nests. But parental misery had no Spock or Salk to state with reassuring certainty that all these woes were minor symptoms of a phase we needn't worry about.

And so we worried constantly.

Could we help these people whom we loved and sometimes couldn't stand? How much would we have to do? How long would it take? Could we do it well? Without resentment? Were we good enough? Would anything be left for *us* when it was done?

There was only Kübler-Ross.

"You wouldn't believe it, Gig!"

Alice—still calling me the nickname from her babyhood—breathlessly announced at my door at ten o'clock one summer night, "It was the most exciting thing!"

She had just come from a session with a Death and Dying therapist who had arranged a conversation for her with an empty chair.

"It was fabulous," she said. "I pretended Mother was in the chair and I told her everything I felt about her dying. I'll practice it some more and then I plan to tell her to her face. Do you think I'm crazy?"

Oh my, yes, I thought. I also thought: Poor thing, you're really scared.

I spent the last two weeks of August at the Jersey shore with my husband Joel, and my sons, Bill and Rich. My parents came down to spend a day. I couldn't wait for them to leave.

The drive was tiring for Mother. While Daddy, Alice, Joel, and the boys went to the beach, she lay, limp as a wet leaf, on a lounge chair on the porch. "My neck is sore," she croaked. "I'm always very tired."

She was so small. So sad. So clearly someone to be treated sweetly. I wanted to . . . and I would have . . . if she only hadn't been so very Mother.

"Do you want tuna fish, egg salad, or cold chicken sandwiches?" I asked near lunchtime.

"Nothing, thanks," she said. "But thanks. I don't want you to go to any trouble."

"Mom, it's made. And it wasn't any trouble."

"Well, thanks, but I don't want to bother you. . . ."

I couldn't keep it in.

"Goddamnit. Can't you just act normal for a change? Can't you just cut out the phony noes when we both know you'll end up asking for 'a little bit,' which means, 'if it is little then it doesn't have to count'? Can't you just accept? Must you suck the pleasure out of everything?"

She looked as if I had kicked her.

I could have kicked myself.

"Well, if you don't mind . . . I'll have just a little tuna fish . . . with a little butter and a little extra mayonnaise on the side."

It isn't only her. My father sits at the table waiting to be waited on. He is so used to being catered to that he takes without apology—almost without awareness—any service

15

anybody offers. He is well mannered. He always thanks. But he never thinks of picking up. Or washing things. Or serving them. Or putting anything away. I wonder what would happen if my mother weren't there to care for him. Would the catering fall to me? I wonder which of them is worse. I wonder when the hell they'll finally go.

"The doctor says he wants more scans," says Mother while she is limping toward the car. "Next week. But don't you worry."

"Don't worry," Mother says again.

September 18 - October 5

"I'm sorry."

We had been waiting more than fifty minutes when the doctor entered midapology. Within five seconds he had said hello, slipped into his seat, scanned the papers on the top of Mother's folder, and started his report. "The tumor has spread again, Mildred. It is in the left shoulder, the right hip, the lower back, and both sides of the chest. Unfortunately, the hormones and the X-ray treatment didn't work."

Slight pause. "I'm really sorry, Mildred." He *was* kind. And Mother, in the middle of her misery, still managed to look grateful.

"What do you suggest?" my father said.

"Chemotherapy, Sy. A regimen consisting of four drugs, two taken orally and two administered I.V."

Her hemlock cocktail would contain Cytoxan—an agent that prevented cell division; two antimetabolites—Methotrexate and Five Fluorouracil (5FU), inhibitors of meta-

17

bolic pathways that were needed for the reproduction of cancer cells; and Prednisone—a cortisonelike drug the doctor hoped would confer a feeling of well-being.

"They are powerful drugs," the doctor said. "They might have powerful side effects." He cited nausea, soreness of the mouth, bowel distress, loss of hair, change in weight and appetite, bone marrow drop, or falling white blood cell and platelet counts as possibilities.

Mother listened this time, wincing at his every mention of a side effect. She was not then, nor would she ever be, a big believer in informed consent. But years of patienthood had taught her to expect that "possibilities" would end up being certainties for *her*.

"What are my chances?" Mother asked, still looking for the odds.

"They're good," the doctor said. "Sixty-five percent of people on this protocol respond."

There was silence for a moment. Then Mother shrugged, straightened up, and said, "I'll do it. My husband and my children want me to."

Whether it was true or not was moot. We three were good excuses.

"When do I begin?" she squeaked.

"Today," the doctor said. "Right now."

She sagged.

My father rubbed her neck. Alice took her left hand, I, her right.

We three would be support.

Mother holds her arms stiff and squeezes shut her eyes while Sherry, the medical technician, searches for a place that feels right, sticks the hypodermic into Mother's rubbery vein, and very gently works it back and forth. She is *very* kind. I am pushing reassurance into Mother's other hand, trying hard to act as if cell-killing drugs seeping into my mother's arm are commonplace. But when the treatment is done I dash into the bathroom and throw up. Then I drive my parents home and afterward, in keeping with my character, I race around in search of books on chemotherapy and its side effects. I overeat all day. I cry and plan precisely how I'll balance Mother's needs with my responsibilities. I write a rough draft of her eulogy. By some minutes after midnight, when the phone rings, I have buried and exhumed her body twenty times.

"I hate to bother you," she said, "but I heard this thump and I went to see. It seems your father fell out of his chair. . . ."

Joel and I raced him to Emergency where they said it wasn't serious and sent him home. But next day, when he blacked out twice and started tilting to the right, his doctor rushed him to Intensive Care.

"Go home," Daddy says to Mother as we enter his cubicle. "I'm fine."

His swollen face and the hospital gown are the same color: chalk white.

"Don't worry about me."

I hear the hiss of oxygen and see the green line on his heart monitor bounce frantically in rhythm with his every restless move. A vein is open in his hand so that adrenalin can be administered quickly, in case of cardiac arrest.

"I'm fine," he said again. "Go home. You just started chemotherapy. You've got to take care of yourself."

Oh, wrong, I think, dead wrong. *I'm* going to take care of her. And of you.

Who's going to take care of me?

The nurses shooed us out. We went to Mom's apartment where I stuffed some things into a bag and brought her back to stay with me until we saw how well she handled chemotherapy and what would happen to my dad.

It was then I started lining up the wounded, started won-

19

dering whom I would choose to save. It was then I started thinking triage.

Mother shook. She lost her appetite. Her dark brown eyes were as wide and frightened as the eyes of the hungry, orphaned children in the CARE ads. Her always misty sentences got denser; she ended every foggy phrase "and so forth." In the mornings she'd remind me to feed Rich. Late afternoon and early evening she'd tell Rich, who had done it twice a day for seven years, "Don't forget to feed the cat." She talked of rags—a favorite theme—urging me, incessantly, to "keep a damp and a damp-dry rag in every room." She begged forgiveness from my furniture and walls a bit less often than she breathed. She drove me wild. And yet not once did she complain.

My father, diagnosed as having had a minor stroke, was plucked from special care and tucked into a semiprivate room, which Mother didn't like at all but, then, what else was new? His voice was weak; it cracked midsyllable. His head hurt and his heartbeat was uneven. He could only sit erect when propped by pillows.

Alice, who popped in for quick visits after work, would press me for the details of their medical reports.
   "Why is Daddy having awful headaches?" she would ask.
   "I don't know."
   "Why don't you ask the doctor?"
   "Why don't *you?* I'm busy."
   I was invariably abrupt and she, consistently, annoyed.
   I made a hundred small decisions every day. "Not once do you consult me," Alice said.
   She was correct. But I could not. I didn't have the energy. I had to do the phony pepping up and the schlepping of my mother every day. I had to reassure my dad. I needed to explain to Joel that making love did not console the way his

20

arms around me, tightly, as though I were a child, did. I had to ask Rich questions about homework and remind him that, though busy, I was not too preoccupied to note the extra time he tried to spend in front of the TV. I had to field the questions all the worried people calling day and night were asking—to which I had no answers. And, worst of all, I had to ask myself: Which one would I save?

Mother would soon be bald, weak, and withering. Dad would be a basket case. How could I attend to her, take care of him, keep Alice at arm's length, and make a life for me?

Mom overboard? Or Dad?

I reeled from feeling ugly things and noble ones at once. I'd see the killing cancer creeping through my mother's tired bones, would pity her, and think, I want to help you. I'd pray my father would make a full recovery and be elated that I was here to be a comfort. And simultaneously I'd think: Why don't you both expire? Die! Right now. I hate your guts—with all my heart—for doing this to me.

To *me.*

I was obsessed, and sorely tired all the time.

I cried in front of anyone without apology or shame. In cafeterias, on elevators, in waiting rooms, and any other place my inner baby urged, I wept. People looked away, uncomfortable to see my private grief. I didn't care. Crying was a way to cope and manners or appearance wouldn't make me give it up.

The resident left word that he would like to meet with me in private. We made a date for three o'clock in the solarium.

"The CVA has left your father with ataxia," said Extern Grumbach, who had arrived with the resident, Dr. Burden.

(CVA—a cardiovascular accident, doctorese for stroke. Ataxia—a loss in coordination of the muscles, especially extremities.)

"He'll probably recover fully, but not for three or maybe six more months."

"But in the meantime," Dr. Burden added, "someone must be with him constantly. Until he walks without support."

They said they couldn't keep him in the hospital much longer.

"My mother started chemotherapy nine days ago and she's not strong," I said. "I'm responsible for both of them. You've *got* to keep him here until I figure out a way to manage."

They were sorry but, unfortunately, firm. "We can't. The hospital will need the bed."

I cried. They only looked a little bit uncomfortable.

"Can't we get him into a rehabilitation center?"

"Not likely. And I doubt that therapy will help. His problem will resolve itself in time."

"But so will everything," I whined.

They nodded.

Another truth, and no solution.

My grim and gray-faced father, wedged between four pillows, wears an ice-filled plastic glove upon his whitened head to ease his pain. He is struggling to feed himself and failing when I walk into his room. Food is falling off the fork; beet stains slowly spread upon the sheet. His cigarette is on the brink of dropping from the ashtray to the table where, without my intervention, it would have surely rolled onto his lap to start a conflagration.

"I'll be right back," I say while smothering his cigarette. "Wait here."

I march through winding corridors until I come to Social Services: bare-walled rooms with dirty tiled floors, forms on every table, signs on every door. I find a social worker who is full of sympathy, and who is really very sorry but my parents aren't poor enough for Medicaid, and Medicare will only pay for rehabilitation in a hospital, not for full-time help at home, which is what, we both decide, they definitely need.

The parents of a friend of mine had saved throughout their lives so they could pay their way when they got old and sick.

"They put money away every week," the son confided. "Since I was young they talked about how important it was to save for a secure old age."

His father had a stroke four years ago. When the hospital could no longer keep him and a nursing home was needed, they learned that the father's nest egg would buy less than half a year of care in a private nursing home, leaving *nothing* for the mother who was ill.

Medicare insurance was no help: the patient wasn't being rehabilitated and there is no reimbursement for custodial care. To be eligible for Medicaid the person getting help must be impoverished.

Within four months, his father qualified.

"Not poor enough for Medicaid," the social worker said.

Just wait.

My diary, September 29: *I will rent a hospital bed, put it in the living room for Daddy, and keep my mother up in Billy's room. If they're still here when he comes home from college at Thanksgiving, he can room with Rich.*

No.

Better put the rented bed in Billy's room and Mother on the sofa in the den.

No.

Rent the bed and let them both go back to their place where I'll stay until the stumbling has stopped.

No.

Oh, help!

Joel wouldn't tell me what to do. He insisted anything I wanted was all right. "If you want to bring your parents here, that's fine. If you think it's easier for you to go to their apartment, that's okay, too. Do what's right for you and don't worry about us."

It was nice of him, but not remotely what I wanted. I wanted him to tell me what to do.

"I hate them both for doing this to me," I'd cry. He would say, "They hate it more than you." Although I knew that he was right, I didn't want to hear what I already knew. I wanted to be told, "It's all right dear." I wanted him to hold me, to say, "Don't worry your little head, I'll handle this. I'll take care of everything."

Some feminist.

I wanted parents.

"Do me a favor," Mother says at breakfast as she slathers butter on a cracker. "Stop at Lord & Taylor on our way to the hospital today so I can get some scarves. My scalp is starting to get cold."

Her part was getting wider every day.

"Let me help you choose a wig," I say.

She makes a face. "Not yet."

"But you should have it. You should start to wear it *before* your hair is gone," I say, not saying bald.

"Not yet."

"We have to stop at Lord & Taylor, so we won't be down until noon," I tell my father on the phone. "How was your night?"

"Not bad."

"And this morning?"

"Not good," he says. "I just fell out of bed."

My friends were blessings. Debbie and Ina made a list of people who would work four-hour shifts to help my father walk when he came home. Mother obviously couldn't do it; Daddy couldn't safely lean on me—he was too big. Alice,

Joel, and Rich would be available on weekends—maybe nights—but not reliably all day.

"You've got family and friends," Debbie and Ina said as they presented me with names. "They want to help. They love you and you're not alone."

Never was I more alone.

But, clearly, I was loved.

Lee, another friend, a movement therapist who used dance as a form of psychotherapy, insisted that the resident was wrong. "I know damn well that physical therapy will help your father regain his strength much faster than mere waiting," she said. "You've got to be assertive. Tell his doctor what the hell you want."

Next morning I was on my knees. "Please," I begged Dr. Binnion. "We need help."

The doctor called a social worker who arranged for an evaluation at Magee Rehabilitation Center. The doctors at Magee agreed to test my father to see if he'd respond to therapy. If so, he'd be allowed to stay. If not, they'd send him back to Pennsylvania Hospital for one more day, and then they would discharge him.

October 4 would be Decision Day. If my father was admitted, I would get to join my husband in Florida, at a convention, for four days away from doctors and disease.

Knock, knock, I prayed. Please let my father in.

"Where's the money?" Daddy said to Mother as the drivers of the cabulance switched him from the stretcher to a wheelchair. They had brought him safely to Magee and now he wished to tip them.

Mother fumbled in her bag. He fumed. She was too slow.

"Goddamn," he barked. "I told you I would want the money when we got here."

Mother stared.

"Isn't that a lot?" I whispered as I saw her push two tens toward him.

She shrugged.

He looked electric chairs at me.

Not until the drivers made prolonged obeisance did I recognize the tens in proper context: potency. Fatigue had made me dense. My mode was neozombie.

Mother, on the other hand, was sharper. Her tremors were intense, which meant she had to concentrate to make the simplest moves. She had been alone at her apartment for a week, doing work and meeting friends and going to the hospital to visit Dad. Everyone was full of praise. And it was amazing to see her grow into her notices; the greater the raves, the more she underplayed brave lady.

My father was depressed or mad or both most of the time, and who could blame him? But the longer he felt sick and impotent the more his self-absorption grew. He rarely asked me about Mother anymore.

Alice, still a client of her Death and Dying therapist, was "dealing with" her anger toward our mother. Mother, she was certain, was the single source of all her woes and only by a superhuman act of will, my sister said, did she not kill her.

A young man wheels my father to a testing room and says we three should wait for someone from the social work department who will be with us soon to do an intake interview.

We wait for twenty minutes.

"Good morning," says a young, white-coated woman, finally. Miss T. "I'm the social worker in charge of your father's case. I'd like to get some family background. Won't you come this way?"

She is dark and doesn't smile. Terribly intense. "My father had a stroke the day my mother started chemotherapy," I tell her as we're walking down the hall. I'm interested in shortening our saga.

"Thanks for sharing that," she says to me. Then, attentively she asks my mother, "Has anything unusual happened in your family these past few weeks?"

Uh, oh, I think. A recent graduate.

Mother breaks into a soliloquy on cancer, chemotherapy, her husband's stroke, his hospital stay, and so on; her staying at my house, how wonderful my husband and my son have been, the way we've all pitched in—including Alice—and so forth . . . and on and on . . . and all this time my sister's foot is pushing on the bottom of my wooden chair to signal me that Mother's rambling makes her feel insane. I try to shove her foot away, discreetly, and to tell her, nonverbally, not to bother me with *her* distress—Mother makes me crazy, too. *I* want to get this over with as much as she and maybe get the hell away.

Miss T., who has nodded sympathetically throughout my mother's solo, uses Mother's gasp for air to shift into the NOW. "What is Mr. Rubin really like?" she wants to know.

"Everybody likes him," Mother says. "He's a lot of fun and when he's well . . ."

T.'s head is bobbing up and down but Alice cannot stand another second of such a public sell. She interrupts. "My father's got a rotten temper. He's miserable to me. We fight like cats and dogs. . . ."

T. gives an assenting shake of head. How well she understands!

Mother, meantime, rages at my sister for this breach of family privacy. She gives her a dirty look. She gets a nod from T. Alice, however, will not shut up. I am mad and getting scared. With all her bobbings of acceptance, I know damned well that this Miss T. does not possess the skill to reassemble families.

"Look," I interrupt in my highest dudgeon tone. "If what you want to know is about Daddy when he's normal, I can tell it."

"Please."

I say he is a flirt, a tease, a cute and sweet man, thoroughly delightful to outsiders, but sometimes sullen, spoiled, and compulsive with his loved ones. "But aren't we all when things are rough?" I add. "And, Miss T., you will agree that these are very trying times for the Rubin family?"

Her busy head replies, Indeed.

Then she turns away from me and leans intently toward my mom.

"Would you like to be involved in Mr. Rubin's physical therapy?"

Mother weighs precisely ninety-seven pounds. Her shakes would rate a seven on the Richter scale.

She answers incoherently and twitches.

My sister picks that moment for my mother's lesson in deportment. "Sit still," she hisses.

"Shut up," I shoot at Alice. And to Miss T., I say, "Will this take a whole lot longer? If Dad is getting in, I've got to catch a plane to Florida."

Miss T.'s eyes grow very wide.

All her training in acceptance cannot hide the shock.

Vacation? Now?

I stare her down.

Yes, *now.*

We never said we were the Waltons.

"You know," said T., the empathy just oozing from her pores, "I may be wrong, but I'm picking up some bad vibrations. I'm feeling tension in the room among the three of you. Feels like some hostility . . ."

My God.

"You're right." I stand. "We're tense and mad and close to cracking up. So please, dispense with messing with our heads and tell us: visiting hours at Magee, the average length of stay, does Medicare pay everything? Can Daddy have a private room? Should we bring a radio?"

The interview was over.

My father stayed.

I got to go away.

October 5 – October 21

Hollywood was hot and not a perfect change of pace: walkways thick with limping seniors; cardiovascular conversation wafting through the air. "My doctor wants a stress test," I would overhear. Or, "She took my pulse and listened to my heart. . . ." There were nasty pools of water around the wheelchair ramps, and siren screams throughout the night. It was not the place to be if you were trying not to think of death.

I was tired and afraid of what I had ahead of me. I spent much of my time in bed, tried to sleep, and couldn't. I was sexually dead and wanted only to be held. And yet, the change of scene refreshed me. Someone made my bed and kept me supplied with fresh towels; the flowers on my breakfast tray were Band-Aids for my spirit.

There were worse ways to be wretched.

"Your father usually does the money," Mother said the night of my return, "but he can't handle it now and I'm too confused. Would you do me a favor and take care of our finances temporarily?"

Don't! my instinct urged. Hire a CPA. But I was flattered by her trust and said yes.

Payments for their rent and telephone were late; bills from druggists for extraordinary drugs were due. Doctors who refused to deal directly with Medicare were agitating to be paid, which meant that getting money *back* from Medicare was added to the list of things I had to do.

But Mother kept no records, saved no stubs. She wrote no checks for "odd" amounts, which kept her charge accounts in total chaos and God knows how many clerks in credit departments horribly confused. "How do you know your balance?" I inquired. "I call the bank on Monday mornings and on Thursday afternoons. They tell me," she replied.

My father's system of accounting—grounded firmly in paranoia—was even worse. So terrified was he that *anyone* would know his balance, he kept the data on deposits and withdrawals in his head.

"Have you got enough to cover these?" I asked the night I took some checks for him to sign.

He scrawled a ragged signature and shrugged. I could have murdered him.

There was undoubtedly no way it could have gone well. In my peculiar economic code it was perverse for children to know their parents' money secrets. Thus I would see what Mother spent on food each week or what my father paid for clothes and feel as if I'd broken a taboo—as if I'd watched the primal scene.

Their "system" was impossible, and once deciphered it laid bare a set of values I despised. X expenditure was stupid, I decided in my wisdom, outlay Y, ineffably absurd. My sister, without question, got too much. Though I knew damned well that it was vile of me to judge them, the knowledge didn't keep me from my outrage. The only decent thing I did while passing icy sentence on their every economic move was keep my feelings to myself.

30

Aunt Bea, my father's sister, spent four hours teaching me how to crack the Medicare code.

I knew that Medicare was federal health insurance for people over sixty-five, but nothing more. Until our time of crisis, vague notions satisfied. But now that I was handling things, I had to know about the benefits we could expect and what costs would not be covered.

I learned that Medicare hospital insurance—plan A—helped pay for in-patient hospital care, in-patient care in a skilled nursing facility, and certain kinds of home health care. Plan B, the medical insurance, helped pay for doctor's services, out-patient hospital services, out-patient physical therapy, and speech pathology services.

In every area of coverage there were specific services that Medicare would pay for as well as items they refused to reimburse—private-duty nurses, for example. Medicare insurance did not always pay the *total* cost of services it covered, and not every doctor accepted as adequate the payment Medicare agreed to make, which meant the patient had to pay the difference.

Aunt Bea showed me how to file for reimbursement. With piles of Sy and Mildred's medical receipts and stacks of 1490s—request for Medicare Payment forms—around me on the floor, government compassion became a lifesaving reality. If either Mom or Dad had been under sixty-five and as sick as they were then, no amount of middle-class respectability would have kept them off welfare.

I was ashamed—am still ashamed—of how I hated going to Magee.

My father shared a six-bed room with a double amputee, two semispeechless victims of strokes, and two other men I couldn't diagnose. Their radios blared jazz and news and sports and rock, at once. In search of quiet I would walk into the visiting room. But there, as if to prove that noise could numb the pain of missing limbs, two television sets shrieked different channels.

Magee exposed some parts of me I could have lived quite happily not knowing.

My father—pink and fat in brown-and-white-checked slacks and brown silk shirt—met me at the elevator. "I walked alone and didn't fall for almost a minute this morning," he would say.

"Great," I'd say. But secretly I'd think: It's come to this, you're proud of what a two-year-old can do.

My father had his arms and legs, which in this hall of horrors was a rarity, and cause to celebrate. He also had an almost gilt-edged guarantee of getting better. But I—locked firmly into *me* and little family circles—could only think: poor thing.

The place abounded with the undaunted, teemed with triumphs of the will and proofs of what the human spirit could accomplish.

What did it do to me?

It made me cringe.

I shivered when my eyes lit on bald stumps, while I thanked God they weren't parts of Dad.

I cut my feelings off each evening as I entered, preferring numbness to my inner screams. Mother came and hovered over Dad.

"Be careful, Sy," she said each time he moved. "Slow down." She tried to light his cigarettes at first, but nearly burned his nose off with her shaking. She cleaned his ashtrays constantly and kept his pockets stuffed with scented tissues she had brought from home. She offered him a cup of water—at five-minute intervals—which she nagged at me or Alice to keep full and icy cold.

Her fussing drove me up the paint-by-number-picture-covered walls.

It seemed to please my dad.

His balance was improving at a rate that meant he might come home within a week.

32

I wasn't happy. Daddy at Magee was Daddy being cared for not by me. Or Mom.

Mother managed well alone. "I'm doing fine," she would say. It was true. She did her housework, met her friends, and made the nightly visit to Magee. But, except for gamely fighting off her nightmares, that was all. She didn't have the pressure of a live-in ailing mate to feel acutely sorry for or worry about constantly. Without my father there to "dirty up the place," Mother could attend to things that pleased her: eating lunch and keeping clean. I knew she would rather die than say so, but his return would mean attention she was not yet ready to pay.

"Maybe you should hire some help," I said.

"No. *I* need to do it."

Housework was her "work." From it came her sense of being useful. "When I can't run my home alone you'll know it's time to call Levine's," she'd say.

Levine's was a funeral home.

What scared her, I was sure, was the care my dad might need, her fear that he was not quite right, and the knowledge that she was marginal herself. Could *she* give a patient home-cooked meals?

"What if I take charge of things when he comes home?" I said. "Just until we're sure you both can manage?"

"Would you? For just a few weeks. Thank you. I'd be very grateful. Thanks."

"Could you come out tonight and help me plan?" I said to Alice. She was pleased. I needed her, and she knew it.

"Of course," she said. "I'll be there."

I got *my* agenda ready, made long lists of *my* suggestions, divided chores the way *I* thought they ought to be.

"Listen, Gig," my sister said as I was spreading all my papers on the kitchen table. "I know how hard this is for you. I want to do whatever I can to help."

"Thanks," I said. "I want you to." I meant it.

33

We turned to business: scheduling ourselves, covering contingencies. "I'll take extra nights," she said. "You'll be there much more than I, so I'll make up for it with evenings."

It was rational and new and very nice: three hours in a room without a fight.

October 15: my last nonangry moment of the month.

Hindsight lets me blame my growing rage and bad behavior on "stress" and "overload," but trendy labels do not get me off the feeling-guilty hook. I was a mess.

Every moment of my life was spent in taking care: early-morning phone calls for my parents' medical reports; rundowns on the things to get "if you have time." I'd drive Mom to chemotherapy, shop for food, cook meals in quantity and freeze them, both for my folks and my own family to cover all the nights I'd be on duty. I paid my parents' bills. I fixed a better system for their Medicare submissions—one that they could follow when I left. I drove, dropped off, took home, and didn't miss a visit at Magee. If Mother had a cough, I went for medicine. If she was weak, I let her lean on me. My father had to have some information on his life insurance "right away." I spent five hours getting it.

The outer me was what their friends described with envy to *their* kids: angelic, the kind of child to make a parent beam. The inner me was someone going nuts.

I was rubbing Mother's bony back while we were waiting for the doctor, I wrote in my diary on October 16. *She moaned "thank you, thank you, thank you," and I kept wondering what would happen if I took the light blue plastic-covered pillow and held it to her face for a few minutes. Would the doctor lie for me?*

I hate Magee, I wrote the following day. *The way the elevator buttons and the water fountains are set low enough for the handicapped. I'm sick of all the handicapped. I hate my father's stubbled cheek. I hate my father, too.*

My mother's constant thanks I saw as symbols of a profound insincerity, my father's *lack* of thanks as proof he took my servitude as due him. My sister was not only getting money, she was getting their permission to be free.

My day of slavery would near its awful end. I'd brave the crush of Philadelphia traffic, double-park, run up to get my mom and walk her down the hall and into the elevator, help her into the car, and head directly for Magee. En route she'd say, "Alice called to find out how I'm doing. Wasn't that sweet of her? She said she might stop by tonight if she has time, but I told her not to push herself. . . ."

I would nod and try to find a parking place. And seethe.

"I can't *stand* the way she talks to waitresses," said Alice. "Extra this and special that. It's sickening."

"*I* used to walk behind her in department stores," I said. "She'd get that voice . . ."

For the first time in our lives my sister and I had more in common than our loathing of each other. Now we had a common enemy: the folks.

"It's okay to tell *me* these things," I said. "But don't you dare let them see *any* of it now. They're much too vulnerable."

I was wise and kind and wonderful—until things came undone the day before my father was discharged.

Someone at Magee, in social work no doubt, had called a meeting of the family to "help cope with the stress of your father's coming home." Alice—having taken the day off—would pick up Mother and meet me at Magee at noon. I arrived alone.

My father waited at the door, somehow managing to pace while sitting in a wheelchair. He was eager to show off his even keel to me and to his fellow patients. "Let's walk through there," he said. He parked the wheelchair in a corner and lumbered eagerly toward Rehabilitation.

He walked the way he lived—impulsively. It drained the

blood from me and someone else, apparently, for a voice across the room called out, "Slow down, for heaven's sake. You're doing fine, Sy, but you've *got* to learn control before you kill yourself."

Fat chance.

Alice burst into the rehabilitation room. It was clear that she was furious with Mom. Mother followed close behind, her face also tight with rage.

"I have to talk to you," my sister whispered. "Now."

We stepped into an alcove.

"I've had it," she declared. "I'm sick of being criticized. I'm up to here with disapproval. I'm sick of seeing them."

Oh, please, I thought. Not now.

I said, "You *have* to stand it and shut up."

"Who says?"

"*I* do."

"I won't."

"Like hell."

"Be still," I said. "Pretend you're civilized."

"Drop dead."

She walked away.

How *dare* she dump on someone as good as me?

Whatever Mother had reported on the argument with Alice was on its way to Daddy's face; each second it was growing redder. We waited in Reception in a silence that grew into a roar, in tension as thick as mud. I couldn't stand it.

"Who *made* this stupid date?" I said.

My sister shook her head. My mother simply shook. My father fidgeted.

The hell with it, I thought. I asked the operator for the social work department and told them we were tired of waiting. I asked them when, if ever, somebody would see us.

Oh dear, said someone very sorry, who begged forgiveness. But there had been some kind of foul-up and there wasn't, at that moment, *anyone* available to check the family coping mechanism.

They didn't know what they had missed.

"Let's pack some of Daddy's things and take them home today," I said. At least we would be doing more than being miserable.

Encased in ice we take the elevator up to five, each of us absorbed in the linoleum. Alice stuffs my father's shirts and socks into a suitcase. Mother pulls them out to pack them right. "Get your father some fresh water," Mother orders me. "I don't want any water," Daddy says. "*I'll* get it," Alice offers.

My body clenches. How dare my mother give commands to me?

My father's forehead vein is going crazy. He is abrupt with me.

I am enraged.

How dare these ingrates act like this, I think. They should be *adoring* me.

"We'd better talk," I say.

We walk into the public room and cram into the only piece of privacy available—a corner.

"You hate me," Mother says before I even have a chance to call the meeting open. "You can't stand me. The only reason you are doing all this taking care is that you feel a sense of duty and you love your father. But I know damned well you hate me and you do not want to do it."

Alice leaps to my defense. "Keep still," my father says. To Mom he says, "Calm down." To me he doesn't say a single word.

I cannot see. My heart is hammering. My sister hears. She tells me to relax and mentions something about family therapy.

How dare she take that tone with me? How dare *she* tell *me* anything?

I look at Mom. Her arms are wrapped across her chest; her lips are a thin line; her body says "keep away." And suddenly I see that she is absolutely right. I *do* hate her. Entirely. My father, too. And Alice.

"Not *want* to do it?" I explode. "How could I *want* to

parent *you?* You never parented me! You all can go to hell,"
I yell above the television's blare. "You've seen the last of
me. Take care of your goddamned selves for a change."

I storm away.

The angel.

All afternoon I swing between disdain for them and self-
disgust. Contempt for me prevails.

"I'm sorry. We're *all* overwrought," I say.

The next morning, when I drive my father home I say—
again—"Forgive me, please."

"Forget it," Daddy answers.

"It's hard for all of us," my mother says. "*I* need to find
somebody I can talk to about cancer."

My sister says, "We need some kind of therapy."

I keep saying, "Sorry."

October 21 - December 12

I developed a routine.

I would arrive at my parents' apartment by midmorning every day and invariably find my mother wiping floors or washing something that it never dawned on me anyone would want to clean: her *hangers*, for example. My father would be dressed in Ultra-Suede and gabardine, pacing, waiting irritably for me to take the walk with him I'd made him promise not to try to make alone. After every morning tiff—"I do not *need* a cane. I'm not *yet* an old man"—we'd head for Rittenhouse Square, he in search of record speed, me entreating, "Slower, Dad. Slow down." We'd arrive back in time to give him lunch and say good-bye to Mother who'd be leaving, guiltily, to meet some friends or just to have some time away. Then Daddy would nap while I planned.

I would pore through cookbooks looking for the dishes that would freeze well, make new lists, scrub and cut the vegetables, make the salad, and have the table set for dinner by midafternoon. I looked efficient. In fact, I was obsessed.

The care did not tax me physically, but the pressure on my head was unrelenting. There were scores of things I did not say: "Don't let the hot water run like that. It uses too much fuel." "Can't you pick up your *own* clothes?" "Why don't you turn the television down?" There were things I couldn't stand to see: my father missing simple words and fumbling for phrases, his weakness, his tilt to the right; my mother's constant fog, her voice, the rags in every room.

"I'd better check with Dr. Daniels. I forgot how many prenisons I have to take."

"It's *Prednisone,* Mother. And it's one three times a day until next Sunday night."

"You're sure?"

"I'm positive."

"I have to send a gift to Ruth and check my Wanamaker's bill. How many prenisons again? I'd better write it down."

Her voice. The talk. The repetition.

And what would I have done to keep away the fear of dying? Smiled nicely?

There was the note from Mother on the counter in the kitchen, thanking us:

> Dear Kids—
>
> We both wish to thank you for all your concern and helpfulness during this most trying period.
>
> You have been a great source of comfort, concern, and love, which has been so greatly appreciated. There have been some scrapes and bitter feelings. Perhaps too much tension. But you have both come through.
>
> A million thanks. I hope you can both tell us to "go to hell" when we feel better.
>
> So much love and appreciation.
>
> Your mother and father.

How typical of Mother to get off a thank-you note no matter what.

("Manners, girls. It only takes a minute and it makes a world of difference.")

How like her to describe our near annihilations as "some scrapes." How fortunate that comfort and concern and love got through.

The note proved Mother knew some of my secrets, too. I wondered if she hated my ambivalence as much as I.

There was the time I walked my father to the doctor. "Can Diane come in the room?" he said. I hadn't asked. I wasn't sure I wanted to.

"Of course," said Dr. Binnion. I went in.

Was Daddy scared?

"What can I do to prevent another stroke?" he said. Apparently he wanted me to hear. Did that mean he was putting me in charge?

There was the hair.

Everywhere in their apartment, that October, frosted strands lay on kitchen counters, bathroom sinks, on gold velvet sofas, and on chairs. Hair clung to every damp-dry rag. It clogged the vacuum cleaner bag I had to change three times a week.

There was uncertainty.

Was this the way their life was doomed to be? The naps? The helplessness? How long could Mother live like this? Should she be so weak? Was she *really* weak or just malingering?

My doubt was nothing new. I had never totally believed that Mother ever was as sick as she had always claimed and now the question—monstrous when applied to cancer—gnawed. Was Mother overacting so she wouldn't have to act?

There was the kitchen.

The spice shelf nearly overflowed with salts and seeds and

sweets. And though it puzzled me that Mom, whose culinary apogee was reached by crumbling salted crackers into Campbell's Chicken Noodle soup, would *need* five jars of saffron, I was pleased. It was a sign of life in that place of desolation.

The knives could not have sliced through peanut butter. The teapot lid fell off each time I poured. The spatulas and serving spoons were buried underneath the napkins, and the coffee languished in a cannister marked "flour." The pasta, cereal, and crackers were so thoroughly embalmed in anti-ant wrap that you would need an Egyptologist to exhume them.

Some of my annoyance came from problems that inevitably arise when a person moves into someone else's space. Mother kept the glasses, for example, where I would have put the plates, mixing bowls where I liked casseroles. But so what? It was what she did with cookware that proved mother was insane.

The gleaming pots and sparkling pans—their shine a never-ending source of pride—were stacked according to their size in spotless cabinets beneath a smudgeless stove. They sat there, their handles glowing and aligned in one direction. And in between them, lest they rub—to buffer them from any mark—my mad mother had put mounds of crisp white doilies!

"Why don't you go home and take it easy?"

Alice would appear at dinnertime on many of the nights she was supposed to be off-duty.

"You go. *I'll* serve dinner," she would say.

No. I had to baste the chicken.

No. I had to warm the bread.

No.

"Why don't you take this weekend off?" she'd say. "*I'll* stay with them."

No.

"Then let me cook some extra meals and do more marketing. . . ."

No. No.

Not for a minute did I kid myself that I was being altruistic. I was simply fighting for control. The reins were mine; I had to hold them tightly, had to keep things running smoothly, running "right." Had to keep my finger in the dike. Even then I knew, acutely, that I trusted only me. While I knew that I was overdoing, I could not believe that anyone could manage as efficiently as I. I wouldn't leave. On those rare occasions when I wasn't there to do the actual taking care, I was so obsessed with making *plans* for running things, it was as if I never left.

No wonder I was exhausted all the time.

The only help I took was from Joel and the boys. Richie did the laundry, set the table, cleared, and cleaned up every night. Billy, off at school, called my parents twice a week without reminder, thereby pleasing them as well as me. Joel moved from not complaining through asking what I wanted him to do to offering specifics and suggestions.

"Why don't you buy some Stouffer's frozen meals instead of cooking every night?" he said. "There's a reason they are called convenience foods."

I wouldn't hear of it.

He held me more than usual. He didn't try to stop my bursts of rage and didn't rub my nose in all the ugly things I said about my parents.

"Thank you. You are acting like a saint," I told him.

"Thank you, Rich." He'd scraped a saucepan clean. "Thanks a lot," I said. "And thanks for emptying the dishwasher, too. I'm really very grateful."

"Will you stop thanking us so much?" My family told me to please shut up. "You've thanked us twenty times in the last hour. You sound exactly like your mother."

Oh.

43

I had feelers out for someone who was good at helping families cope with stress. My father didn't seem to care about it, but Mother wanted someone who "knows something about cancer." Alice was enthusiastic. "Great! But try to find a specialist in dying!"

Through the grapevine came the name of Miriam Shore, a psychologist whose specialty was cancer patients and their families. We met, for the first time, in late October.

It was a good decision.

"Hello. I'm Miriam."

A glow suffused the room when she appeared.

"Come in."

Her rosy cheeks gave off a healthy shine. Everything about her gleamed: gold bracelets circled slender wrists; rings surrounded fingers neatly manicured and polished. Her violet cashmere sweaters were my mother's favorite color; her shoes were Andrew Geller and brand-new. Her voice was soft, her smile was wide and warm. Her perfume—Shalimar! If God had wanted to create the perfect therapist for Sy and Mildred Rubin, He would have made a Miriam Shore.

Mother looked at her approvingly and then at me and Alice with a glance that said, See what you can do if you take time? My flirty father looked delighted. Alice looked abashed at me and I, ashamed, at her. We both were wearing jeans.

"Diane gave me some background," Miriam said to Mother. "But why don't you begin?"

Thus opened session number one: Mother gushing, Alice interrupting, Daddy mostly silent, and me trying to appear as if I didn't need to be in anything called "therapy."

By then I knew my mother's litany by heart. "I'm going to fight," she would say. "I've got to beat this thing. I'd rather die than be a burden." Every day since last September she had been playing variations of this positive-thinking tape. I didn't have to listen.

44

Miriam asked about her past.

"I was a miserable child," Mother said. "Always sick and always whining. No one liked me very much. . . ."

She was the next to youngest of seven children. Her mother, Jennie, had married Fred, an erratic man who drank too much and periodically appeared on the scene to scream and threaten violence. Fortunately, his second most redeeming quality was that he rarely bothered to come home. The first was that he made a lot of money.

"We had a shiny, chauffeur-driven limousine," said Mother. "The driver liked me. He would wait while I went shopping. One time I bought fifteen pairs of kidskin gloves. Another day I bought *two* leopard coats. It was right before my father lost his money in the Crash. . . ."

"Talk about your cancer," Alice blurted.

"Ssh, let your mother talk."

"My mother didn't like me much," my mother said. "My sister, Ethel, was her pet. But I was always good to her. I used to call her twice a day."

She looked accusingly at me. Before my paramedic days I'd adamantly refused to phone her more than four times weekly.

"And lie to her," I said, remembering how Mother wouldn't dare tell her mother anything about the card games. "Your mother must have thought you saw an awful lot of movies."

"Let your mother talk," said Miriam.

"I'm afraid I've doomed my daughters," Mother said. "I dread the thought of passing cancer on to them."

"Don't be silly," said my father.

"Please . . . let her speak."

As if she could be stopped. A monologue, a soliloquy, a flood that Mother couldn't stop until the time was up.

Before we left, Miriam, as part of her summation, made this observation: "I'd like to see a better balance in the family. Diane is overcarrying."

I couldn't wait until our next appointment.

"Why don't you ever *listen?*" Daddy screams at Alice.

"Maybe if you didn't yell so much I would," she shrieks back.

They escalate. Twice they nearly come to blows, and all the while my mother acts like Norman Vincent Peale. "I *know* that I will beat this thing," she chants.

I sit there wondering what *I'd* answer to the question Miriam has just asked Alice: "What do you want from your father?"

From my father? Protection, I guess.

But it's from Mother I need something now.

I want mothering.

I am forty-three and what I really want is a mommy to take care of me.

My God. Does anybody ever get enough?

I cry a little, but no one notices. They're busy with themselves. And Alice.

Mother started changing after session number two. She, who cringed and cried her way through conflict all her life—"I can't *stand* it anymore," she used to scream when Alice and I were only warming up—began to sit, drug-bloated hands clasped placidly, and gaze serenely on us all. It was as if she finally knew that battles were beside the point, that being there was more important than anything we fought about.

Now she showed a new approach to problems. Instead of wringing her hands or saying something mean, she would interrupt an ugly fracas to ask Miriam, "How can we get them to stop? What should I do to help?"

She was acting so out of character that I couldn't reconcile her new persona with the parent who had taught me all I knew about in-fighting. The other mother was a pro at going for the jugular and the psychological crotch. In arguments, my mother could intuit what would nearly kill and use it ruthlessly if she were furious enough. And now she wanted only to negotiate a peace.

No one *I* called Mother talked like that.

My father opened up gradually and just a little. It was hard for him to talk about his feelings. But even with a small emotional vocabulary he managed, intermittently, to talk about an icy, overrighteous father whose approval he could never win, and a mother, two sisters, and half a dozen aunts who had adored him.

Miriam was unseduced.

"You've been indulged and pampered much too long, Sy. Your family needs you now. They need you to be strong and more involved."

A laundry hamper was to be the emblem of my father's major change. To be strong and more involved he promised to pick up his socks every morning instead of leaving them for Mother.

"I want to skip next Saturday at Miriam's," Alice said. "There's a conference at the Civic Center—'Women's Mental Health Concerns'—and I'd like to go. Okay with you if I don't come?"

Okay?

It would be the three of us.

There would be no butting in, no blunted questions about death, no fights.

Okay?

"Okay."

Mother, moon-faced from the steroids, opened our next session. "I feel rotten but I'll beat this thing. I *have* to live. I want to enjoy my family."

"Stop," I interrupted, crying.

So much for Alice's soothing absence.

"What the hell is going on in this family? How come both of you are acting strange?"

"Your parents are growing up," said Miriam. "Now, if they will let Alice grow up . . ."

Alice again.

I started to sob.

47

"But I'm worried about Diane," said Miriam.

People didn't worry about me.

"Really. I'm worried about Diane. She's been taking care of both of you so long—emotionally since she was very little, and lately . . . all the physical care."

Acknowledgment was sweet but very short for *they* were worried about Alice's rent increase and . . .

"Stop," said Miriam abruptly. "How do you feel?" she said to me.

My mother answered.

"Listen to *Diane*," my guardian angel said. "Listen to your older daughter for a change."

I cried.

"I'm really worried about her," Miriam said.

Keep worrying, I wanted to say. I love it.

Miriam moved me to a leather stool in front of Mother.

"Can you touch her?" she asked Mom. "Can you try to give her comfort? She could use a lot of mothering."

"That's easy," Mother said.

It couldn't have been easy. She didn't like to touch. She used to pull her hand away from my young clutch the minute that we reached a curb. She never hugged. It *couldn't* have been easy, but she did it. She rubbed my back and smoothed my hair. I kept crying. I loved it and I couldn't get enough.

"She needs to know you love her," Miriam said.

"I love her very much."

She kissed my head.

"Can *I* get in the act?" my father asked.

"You're too sexy, Sy," said Miriam. "Wait. *They* need to have this time."

She knew that, too.

"What happened yesterday at Miriam's?" my sister asked.

"It was wonderful," I said. "Mother loves me and she

rubbed my head. What happened at the Mental Health Conference?"

"It was great! The Death and Dying workshop was the best. I pretended I was lying in a coffin. . . ."

Five weeks of family therapy did not a model family make. Despite the loving moments there was much old and secret stuff stirred up through which we fought and yelled and felt ashamed. But a core of family strength and family caring was revealed. Now and then I found that I was proud to be related to the people I had tried so hard to be apart from all my life. Sometimes I didn't want to be an outsider.

I didn't even try to keep what we were doing secret and *I,* who had always taken pride in being anti-trendy, started announcing at every opportunity, "My mother asked for cancer counseling. We're getting Death and Dying family therapy."

I spouted all the fashionable phrases: "Death with dignity," "Kübler-Ross," "hospice," and "Brompton's cocktail."

I was ashamed of being au courant, but not slowed down. It was as if I couldn't stop. I had a schtick: "My mother's dying better than she lived," I'd say. "She's given me permission to be happy. I'm very proud of her."

I meant it.

I also came to see that Mother's tragedy included more than pain and suffering; it was the stuff of my projected book.

I consoled my mother when she ached. But I wrote about her symptoms with detachment, too. I needed to be sure my notes were right. Careful note of each complaint might help me recreate a certain time. Records might reveal a pattern I could later write about reacting to.

More guilt! Mother's anguish, which I tried to ease, was also what I needed as creative yeast. Mother's tragedy, suffering, and pain were now my raw material.

My God! How selfish could I be?

I decided not to have Thanksgiving dinner. Even though I had hosted it for the previous five years, and though the cooking was traditionally shared, the mere thought of renting chairs for thirty-three was overwhelming. I canceled.

"Do me a favor," Mother said one mid-November morning.

"Favors" used to be commands. I stiffened.

"I'm not trying to blackmail you . . . and it's okay if you say no . . . I really mean it."

Something in her voice lowered my defenses.

"If I can."

"Would you have Thanksgiving dinner? It may be my last Thanksgiving and I'd like to be with everyone this year. I'll be glad to help."

At her *peak* of health my mother's contribution to a family meal had been three jars of olives.

"Just come," I said.

It was a splendid, friendly family feast. We prayed in memory of Uncle Wolf, who had died last spring, and for my parents' health. Daddy overate. Mother sat, like Buddha, on the sofa in my living room. The once sleek and slender body was round enough to bounce and her legs resembled redwood stumps. She told me of the "kindness" Daddy did that morning. Worried because she had been asleep so long, he came into her room, bent down to see if she was breathing, and kissed her on the cheek. This kind of sweetness was new for him, new for both to have between them, and nice Thanksgiving news for me.

The little naps my mother took midafternoon had stretched from after lunch until six o'clock. Her appetite, except for sweets, was waning. Her head, back, and shoulders ached; her cough was thickening. Often she was short of breath. Her abdomen felt strange. "Not pain exactly . . . kind of an

50

awareness." The television and the radio, always on "for noise" or "company," were set to screaming volume. Mother couldn't hear.

The doctor said it was a respiratory problem. I decided she was dying.

I was terrified: of Mother's dying, of Mother's dying soon, of Mother's living out her time as miserable as this, of the pressure on my father to live with anyone as sick as she.

One day while Mother slept and Daddy lay on the sofa, I said, "You've got to get some exercise. You ought to go outside and take a walk." But it was cold. A walk through whipping winds would not help angina. "At least you've got to change your walls," I said. *I* could get away when I went home at night.

"It's hard for you," I said, hoping that acknowledgment would help head off another heart attack.

"It *is* hard," he said. "Not knowing what will happen is difficult and now it's hard another way. Mother has started coming into my room and sleeping with me the last few nights. I guess she's scared . . . and I want to comfort her . . . but I'm not getting any sleep."

On December 4, the doctor didn't like the sound of things. "Bring her in. We'll fit her in."

Daddy was still sleeping when I got to the apartment. Mother hadn't finished dressing; she wasn't strong enough. I fixed the buttons on her blouse and zipped her skirt. She was coughing hard and often. Between coughs she took gasping, shallow breaths.

It took forever walking to the elevator.

"I didn't think it would end like this," said Mother. "I didn't think it would be as rough."

"You're not in pain?"

"No . . ."

The elevator came. I helped her find a place among the passengers and tried to keep from crying, but I couldn't. Mother didn't see. The others did and looked away.

51

"I didn't used to care," she told me in the car.

"About what?"

"If I died. I didn't used to care. But now I want to live. I love the closeness with my children and my husband. I want to savor it."

I rubbed her hand.

"I don't want to be a burden," Mother said.

She wasn't.

She waited in room six, almost asleep. She was so racked with coughing, so very tired. I cried. She didn't hear. Barbara, Dr. Daniels's medical assistant, entered just to check, saw my tears, and brought me tea, which didn't change a thing but made a world of difference. We moved Mother to the examining table where she might sleep more comfortably while waiting.

"Are you crying?" Mother said.

"Yes," I said. "I'm worried about you."

I rubbed her cheek, caressed her back. The touching wasn't awkward anymore. It felt just right.

"It feels so good," she said.

It did.

The doctor listened as I ran down Mother's list of symptoms, examined her, ordered rest, a chest X-ray, cough medicine, and Ampicillin.

"I'm certain that the cough explains your weakness," he said. "I know you're worried about cancer, Mildred." He had to shout. "But *infection* is the culprit here—not cancer."

"You mean I'm going to get better?" Mother whimpered.

"I guarantee it."

You could see her spirits lift, but they couldn't stay aloft beyond the next attack of coughing.

No wheelchair was at hand. With Mother leaning on my arm, I walked us to the X-ray waiting room. It was full of people who looked at her and looked at me and very quickly looked away.

Mother was too frail, too much like tissue paper. She looked too weak to be alive for long. I wept.

"Such a comfort . . . such a comfort," Mother whispered as we waited for the clerk to call her name.

"What?" I knew. But I wanted her to tell me.

"You . . . the way you're here and soothing."

Her hand was warm and small. I wanted her to tell me everything.

"I think your father is scared to death I'm dying," she said as we were driving home.

Me, too.

And I was tired. I could take it for a little while longer. But how much longer?

She got worse. The killing cough continued. An effort of four steps would make her sigh and groan. Still she wanted to do things herself. She dragged a stool to the kitchen sink where she sat and scrubbed the breakfast dishes. Three plates, two mugs, some spoons and forks took fifteen minutes. Then she would need my help to get to bed. Her hearing leaked away; the radio blared, reminiscent of Magee. We had to yell to connect. She walked bent over, as if she wanted to be wrapped around herself. I couldn't stand to see her or be with her. I couldn't stay away.

I was tired and in need of sleep and even more in need of being somewhere else. It seemed unfair that I—so healthy and so full of life—should have to give away *my* good time.

"But if you weren't in your prime you couldn't do this half as well," said Ina. "Your parents are lucky to have you."

True.

And me them.

In some peculiar way, caring for them was a kind of grace.

December 12 – January 2, 1979

"The cough is worse. She's weaker. She's very short of breath." By now I called the doctor every day.

"Get her right in," he said briskly. "I'm concerned."

The blood test showed a red cell count of eight. Twelve was normal for a woman. "Anemia," the doctor said. "I want her in the hospital."

"I want to stay with her," I said. "She's scared."

"That's a good idea, Diane," said Dr. Daniels. "I'll order a cot and write permission on her chart for you to stay."

That clinched it. That meant he knew she was dying, too.

Everyone agreed that Daddy shouldn't stay alone. Suppose he dropped a cigarette? What if he collapsed and no one knew? Reluctantly he said he would sleep at his sister Emily's.

"But maybe *I* should stay with Mother at the hospital," he said. That newly tender quality again—the sweetness. He really wanted to be near her, but to see him squirming in a chair would not have helped my mother heal.

"You've got to take care of yourself," I told him. "So does she. She'd see you being restless, she would worry and . . . please . . ."

He stayed at Emily's.

I packed my bags and hugged Rich who had a cold, a cough, and, for the past three days, some neck lumps that we thought meant mononucleosis. Joel couldn't take him for the blood test the next day—he'd be out of town—so I said I would do it in the afternoon. That I didn't ask a friend to do it for me in that time of crisis was not unusual. In any near catastrophe I become not only wholly focused, but fully energized. I tackle every task as if the more I do the better are the chances of a miracle, as if the more I move the less I will feel fear.

This time—in keeping with my character—I planned to comfort Mother, keep her Anastasia act from alienating nurses, arrange for Daddy's mental ease, screen calls and company, make sense of what the doctors said, and care, with love and patience, for my son. In keeping with my character disorder.

I made the narrow cot and moved it next to Mother's bed. Every fifteen minutes someone came to take her blood or blood pressure. Mother didn't mind. She wasn't well enough to label them annoying interruptions. To me they seemed like acts of grace from a staff of saints who got her through the night. Technicians crooned apologies while trying to coax blood from Mother's flaccid veins; nurses said just tell them if we wanted anything; the resident appeared three times—once merely to reassure.

"We don't know what it is yet . . . maybe by tomorrow. But we are keeping a careful eye on things. Try not to worry."

I'd listen to her labored breaths and wait. Every time the

55

cough woke her I would hold her tight. I saw my task: to keep the cough from tearing her in half.

"It's so good to know that somebody you love is here," she said.

At night she was all moans and sighs.

"Thank you, thank you, thank you," every time I rubbed her back.

She was swollen all over, yet, somehow, bony.

"Are you warm enough? Why don't you try to sleep?" she would ask.

I alternately cried and felt elated.

I thought of Uncle Wolf who died without his wife or children near because the staff in the cardiac care unit sent his family home with a promise they would call in case of any change in his condition, and they hadn't. Despite his long and rich and good and loving life, his death without a loved one near him haunted his survivors.

Envy me, I thought. After all the fury and the fights and the wishing she were different and resenting everything she did and didn't do, I'm here. I'm glad. I'm lucky.

Then I would cry. Don't die, I'd think. I'm scared. I don't want to be without you and I'm frightened. It will hurt and you're so breakable. I don't want to see it.

I sobbed.

Mother couldn't hear.

On the morning of day two the doctor had a tentative diagnosis: autoimmune hemolytic anemia, which meant that Mother's body was destroying its red blood cells. She was to stay in bed, breathe oxygen, be given steroids intravenously, and wait. Blood was being taken regularly. We'd have to see. . . .

"Would you help me bathe?" she asked me when the doctor left the room.

"Of course."

She was so weak. "Did you bring the body lotion? Would

you rub it on my arms?" She was so vain. "Is my mirror here?" She wanted lipstick, perfume, rouge. "Would you help me with the light blue lacy nightgown?"

She was still Mildred.

Alice called.

"It was wonderful to be here," I reported. And, full of generosity, I offered *her* the chance to spend the night with Mother.

"It really was superb," I said.

In the careful, rounded tones one uses for the feeble-minded, Alice talked to me:

"Thanks, Gig. But I don't mind missing the opportunity. I'm glad to let you do it if you like."

She hung up very quickly.

Miriam called. "Try not to overdo," she said. "This can go on for a very long time." She wanted us to come on Saturday, "Even if your mother has to be alone for a few hours. There is so much stress . . ."

Daddy arrived. He said he hadn't slept. Mother told him to go home and not to worry anymore.

"I'm not dying now," she said.

I took Richie to the lab and raced back to the hospital.

Her count went down to seven, which was bad. But it stayed at seven for eight hours, which was good.

"We need stability right now," the resident said.

Teams of experts came to see my shrinking mother lie there like a frightened little girl who hoped that if she weren't difficult the pros would like her and would try to make her well.

The lumplike way with doctors, the mental fog, the hateful whine were there as usual—*italicized*—if anything. But now they seemed of little consequence. For once I didn't hate her for her passivity. What mattered was my mother's life. What mattered, too, was that—at last—my love for her was clear and whole. For once I didn't feel ambivalent.

Five days and fifty blood tests later they said the problem was only a blood abnormality associated with infection.

Mother would recover.

The three of us at Miriam's sans Mother discussed "what ifs." There was a lot of wanting to pin down, make plans; a lot of wondering how long and what we should expect. All we had were questions: questions that betrayed impatience, questions we were too ashamed to ask outside that setting, and questions that we knew damned well nobody had the answers to—but which we couldn't keep from thinking all the time. The three of us at Miriam's: we didn't seem like a *family* without Mother.

On the morning of day six someone from Audiology reported on the hearing test.

"You'll have to get a hearing aid," a lady talking loud and mouthing syllables informed my mom. "You have a permanent loss of hearing caused by age."

"Baloney," Mother said. "I'm not that old. And the wig would get in the way of any hearing aid. Get out."

On the morning of day seven she said, "I think I can wash myself now. Not fast . . . but I think I can do it alone."

An advance for her. At last.

For me? Back to ambivalence.

My diary from December 21: *I didn't go to the hospital today. Stayed home and cooked for the freezer. Richie has mono. Mother is weak but getting better. Billy will be home from school tomorrow for two weeks. We're not going to take the cross-country ski vacation in Vermont that I had planned.*

I hate it all again. I am tired of my parents, tired of my

58

sister, tired of the caretaking. I'm wishing not only for vacation, but just as much—or more—for the mental freedom I would need in order to go anywhere but to the hospital.

I hate the way that everything is tentative.

Mother mends. But what does she get well for? Nothing fits. The life she spent so many years despising she is now greedy to extend. The quality of life is irrelevant to her—no matter what she says. It's only quantity that counts.

How am I to live a normal life? What are sane arrangements? Should we get help at home for them, even though Mother doesn't want it? I know she needs to feel she's gaining, that she is in control, productive. But what am I to do?

How am I to free my head? All I do is think about them all the time. And me.

This is too hard. Every day I have to hack out a new path. In the beginning, I only thought I'd have to take a little hike. I wish she had died. I wish she would get on with it so I can go on living. I wish I'd have her here forever. I wish I thought the same thing three minutes in a row.

"I can't come home," she said.

"Why?"

"I'm running fever."

"Why?"

"Dr. Daniels said you should page him as soon as you get here."

"I don't know why she has a fever now," the doctor said. "But I don't like it. The heavy dose of cortisone she's been getting should have suppressed any temperature elevation. She has to stay until it drops. I don't think it's serious. We'll take it day by day. And, as long as she's staying, I've ordered bone and liver scans."

Poor Ma.

Wearing pantyhose and walking shoes and a knee-length cotton gown that ties in the back, she sits despondently on an orange vinyl chair. She must have stopped preparing to come home mid-rouge: her right cheek is pink and even, but the left has three bright, unconnected dots.

She cries.

"I feel so bad," she says.

"You must be horribly disappointed," I say.

"That isn't it. I feel so bad for all of *you*," she says. "For you, for Daddy, and for Alice. I don't want you to worry. I don't want to be a burden."

It is part guilt, I think. It is the kind of thing that women understand. They know what illness does—the time it takes, the energy, the interruption of the flow of things, the inconvenience, the way it leads to rage.

I bet it also is part dread. Does she fear I've learned that the literal translation of "I don't want to be a burden" is "I hated taking care of my sick parents and I'd rather die than have my child feel like that toward me?"

Poor Ma.

Was I sending out resentment signals? God knows I was ambivalent again and tired, feeling lost in thanatology.

"Am I doing anything to make you feel that I think you are a burden?"

"No." She weeps.

"What is it, then?"

"I'm scared."

"Of what?"

"You'll leave me."

She couldn't look at me. I held her and we rocked. "I won't abandon you. I'll be here and take care of you as long as you need it, Mom. I promise."

I meant it. But God, I was so tired, and so sick of taking care.

The scans were "a mixed bag," the doctor said. The cervical spine remained unchanged. "There *might* be some abnormal liver cells." We'd see. The bone scan showed two small new areas of spread—the right pelvis and the cheekbone. "Barely detectable, not significant." But there.

We decided since the evidence of spread was slight and Mother was so frail we wouldn't tell her if she didn't ask. She didn't ask.

She was discharged on December 29. Blood level up and stabilized. Fever down. Hearing more. But very weak and "needing care."

"Please don't hire anyone," she pleaded. "I'll be strong enough to manage soon."

New Year's Eve. My summing up:

I'm numb. I can no longer cry. Even though I know this time next year I'll be without a mother.

I'm forty-three and I feel completely done. My energy has disappeared.

All I'm left with is a tic in my right eye.

January 2 - February 8

"I don't look like myself anymore."

She wore an old brown raincoat. Torn stockings bagged around her knees. One hand held a cane, the other a handbag and some newspapers. Her wig was too big; it shifted on her scalp.

"I look exactly like my mother did a month before she died."

She looked exactly like a candidate for a vagrancy citation, a bag lady.

"You look fine," I lied.

We were on our way to chemotherapy, and I was trying to get Mother to be clear about her symptoms.

"Why don't you make a list?" I said. "That way you could cover everything."

"I can't."

"Then tell me. *I'll* make it."

"I'm tired of telling you how miserable I am."

"I don't mind. And the only way the doctor can help you is if you are precise. So tell me again—what *kind* of pain did you have in your legs the other night?"

"I told you. The kind that Hitler should have had."

"You're doing well, Mildred dear," the doctor said. "Take the Prednisone and Cytoxan through Saturday, then stop. I'll see you in two weeks."

"Why do I still feel so lousy?"

"You were very, very weakened. It will take some time, but you will feel better. I promise."

"I'm feeling good today," she said on January 17.

Her only outing was for chemotherapy. She slept twelve hours at night and had to nap each afternoon. She struggled to get out of chairs, couldn't walk without a cane, often didn't bother to get dressed. Her fingers tingled constantly. Her neck was stiff. Her back and legs were sore.

That, by then, was good.

"I think you can stop coming every day," she said.

I thought I was delighted.

I thought I'd get my house put right and then I'd organize my notes. I'd make an outline and begin to write. I'd spend some time relaxing first. I'd read, see some friends, and definitely go skiing in Vermont. . . .

I must have thought I was somebody else.

Instead of easing out I nearly drowned in being indispensable. I started cooking furiously. I bought and stirred and spooned great gobs of all the sweet and creamy things my mother loved to eat into dozens of new Tupperware containers. I called three times a day and popped in unannounced to offer help. "Is there anything you need? Anyplace you want me to go?" It no longer mattered that I didn't like to drive.

Once more I was assumed to be an angel. But it didn't

have a thing to do with being good. I was addicted.

Taking care took choice away. It imposed a structure on my life; I always knew precisely what I had to do and, even if I hated it, I didn't have to struggle with decisions. I didn't really *have* to write a book about attending to my parents. I was exempted from confronting empty pages by the alibi built into my assignment: No one asked about the status of my manuscript; it was a given that anyone so busy didn't have the time to write. I was treated with extra deference by my friends, my family. Joel defused many fights we would have had if things had been normal.

I didn't know this then. I only knew it didn't matter that my mother said I should stop coming every day. I couldn't stay away.

My tic got worse. My lower back was sore. I made a date to meet with Miriam, alone, one day late in January.

"I haven't cried since that night in the hospital when I thought Mother was dying," I said. "I'm numb and bored."

"You're beat," said Miriam. "Your body and your face are tight. You look like hell."

"I've lost my spark," I whined. "This stuff makes you old. By the time I'm done with taking care of them the fun will all be out of me and *I'll* be nearly dead."

So much for Sy and Mildred's little seraph.

"What would happen if you disengaged?"

"Mother would feel abandoned and Daddy would die without someone to take care of him."

"That's dumb," she said.

She said I should let go, back off.

"But who is going to take care of them?"

"Themselves. Your sister. Others in the family . . ."

"Not me?"

"Of course. But not exclusively."

"But Mother—"

"Mother yourself."

"It takes so long," I said. "And once you get out of a crisis, everything goes flat. I do fine in the excitement and the drama, but not this."

"You'd better work on easing off," she said. "And you'd better take care of yourself. It can go on like this for very, very long."

I didn't ask the doctor how much time my mother had. I, who used to gather facts and propound questions just to numb myself, to keep away anxiety, suddenly turned dumb. It was as if my ignorance protected me. Suppose the doctor told me Mom had *years?* Would I have read that as an indeterminate sentence for myself? Would I have cracked? Perhaps I needed the uncertainty to keep me on the edge, to make me stay alert. Or maybe I assumed the doctor didn't know. Or wouldn't tell. At any rate, I didn't ask. I just assumed that Mother's death was imminent.

If she slept and wanted sweets—sometimes hepatitis symptoms—I was sure the cancer had spread to her liver. If she lost a pound, it meant she was shriveling. A headache aspirin couldn't cure, I took as evidence of brain tumor.

One of the things that nagged at me was knowing that if *I* had been as sick as she I would have scoured the world to find a cure, or begged someone to do it for me. Was I, I wondered, doing everything I could for Mom? Here she was, dependent on her doctor, and, indirectly, but without a doubt, on me, and I had arranged no consultations at Sloan-Kettering. Nor had I asked for vitamin C in megadoses, or thermal therapy. I had simply gone along, passively, like Mother.

I started torturing myself. Was fatigue preventing me from taking her to doctors who were doing innovative things? Was she a candidate for anything experimental? Did I think that saying, "Let's see other doctors," would undermine her faith in Roger Daniels? Or had I—quite unconsciously—decided not to slow down the process?

I asked my father if *he* felt we ought to call in a consultant. He said he wasn't sure.

"Maybe you should talk to Dr. Daniels," he suggested.

I tried to figure out a way to pose those awkward questions—fast—to busy Dr. Daniels on the phone. I ended up deciding I should write. But after seven tries I still sounded as if I didn't trust his judgment. Only as a last resort did I think to ask the source.

"I've thought a lot about it," Mother said, "but I don't want to schlepp around the country. I trust Dr. Daniels. He knows about the new techniques and he's told me he will use them if he thinks the chemotherapy is not working. Besides, he promised not to let me suffer."

It was just a tiny mental step from worry over cancer, chemotherapy, and cardiovascular disease to an obsession about death. By January I had crossed the line, and my timing coincided perfectly with the Zeitgeist. Death was everybody's hang-up then! Books full of information about dying were pouring off the presses. One put dying in historical perspective; another taught you how to talk to people who were terminally ill. I learned about bereavement, and denial, and acceptance, and depression, and compassion....

Day after day I read through all the books and never quite believed that there were people who had "come to terms" with being dead, that there were those who glowed with the knowledge they would soon cease to be. I wondered if the jargon was not a way of masking fear or marking time. Could anyone look death directly in the face? Not I.

I scored twelve on a "Check Your Fear of Death" test that appeared one Sunday in a supplement. "If you score between eleven and fifteen," the author wrote, "you are extremely frightened." With one eye on my psyche and the other on my sister's necrophilia that I'd been making fun of for so long, I registered to take a course at a local Y. For sixty dollars I would be "Talking About Death, Dying,

66

and Loss" on ten consecutive Tuesday nights.

I wanted to talk about death all the time. If I had had my morbid way I would have taken up all the slack in Mother's waning life with questions about ends. "Do you want to will your eyes, Ma?" I would have liked to ask. "Would you like to die at home? What should I do about your funeral? What about your eulogy?"

I fantasized the deathbed scene: jewelry divided—the cherished pearls to me—the family holding hands and listening to what she now knew was true. No more talk about clean rags. Just lucid summings up.

I tried to keep my death obsession quiet, but now and then it got the best of me.

"We're going cross-country skiing from the second to the seventh," I announced. "I plan to call you every night at seven."

"Go. Don't worry. There's absolutely nothing wrong with me."

"Mother," I screamed. "Don't be crazy. You are very seriously ill."

She needed my reminder.

There was the time I'd brought some groceries down, plunked them on the kitchen counter, looked around, and saw myself in Mildred Rubin's antiseptic Eden: rags were soaking in ammonia; the vacuum cleaner waited to be run; here was cleanser, there a mop; the brush was for the bathroom. For a moment I realized how much I'd miss the scouring scenes when Mother died.

I had to say it: "I hope you get a nice clean place in heaven when you're dead, Mom."

Mother, on the other hand, was expressing her will to live in everything she did. Each day she grew more direct, more greedy for everything she wanted right away.

"I'd like something new," she said in answer to "What can I do?" "I want something . . . I don't know. . . ."

"A pretty blouse?"

"No . . . I don't think so."

"A dress?"

"Nope."

"A sweater? Skirt? A robe?"

"I know . . . I'd like new sheets."

"Okay." I said I would get them.

"Would you bring them over to me today?"

"I'd rather not. I want to work and I have to pick up Rich and make dinner. . . ."

"Could Joel drop them off on his way to work tomorrow morning?"

Certainly.

I called her from the store to check on color. Beige was fine.

"Would you bring them over this afternoon?" she asked again.

"No," I said.

"Okay." Her voice was small.

"*No.* I don't *want* to drive into town now. I'm too busy."

"Okay."

It was not okay. There was no way it could be called okay. If she had died the following day that "no" would have been with me forever. How the hell was I supposed to back off?

Despite the ever-present pangs of guilt and constant fear that each day was Mom's last, I was no longer at her constant beck-and-call; I was starting to refuse to do some things. I was planning a vacation and I wouldn't try to stop my mother from working herself into a collapse.

"She pushes much too hard. You ought to stop her," her friends said.

"If I can't be useful I would just as soon be dead," she said. She would vacuum a small area of carpet, stop and rest, make a portion of a bed, take a break. "I figured out a way to do the kitchen floor," she told me proudly. "I sit on a

68

stool, put two soapy rags down, and scrub it with my feet."

Her cane would be a pusher in the bathrooms.

Mother—of necessity—invented.

She became increasingly demanding. She wanted special foods.

"Daddy's picking up vegetable soup for me from Bain's. Would you please buy two pounds of cinnamon buns from Viking Pastry and bring them over or send them with Joel in the morning?"

Could Alice cook her some chicken parts? And maybe—when I had the time—now that I wasn't coming to the apartment so often—could I try this recipe she had cut out of *The New York Times?*

She had an army on the streets. She, who always swore she never asked a friend to do a favor, now had troops all over town. One battalion went for Harvard beets to Horn & Hardart, another for croissants from the French bakery. Deployment was frequently a problem. More than once did mother duplicate an errand.

Amazingly, no one but me said no.

Joel, Bill, and Rich had come with us to Miriam's a few times. I had wanted my sons to see their family as capable of change, wanted them to be imbued with a sense of multi-generational love and multigenerational duty. Unfortunately, we usually argued when they were there.

This time all was calm. Mother talked about how much she ate, how many sweets. She said she wondered if living was worth it anymore.

"Do you really mean that?" Miriam asked.

"I guess I don't," said Mother. "I'm still taking che-motherapy, so I must want to live. I get a lot of pleasure from my family, but things are getting awfully hard."

"Why don't you consider getting help?" asked Miriam.

"No way. When a maid comes into my house, it'll be time

to call Levine's," she said. "If I can't be useful, I might as well be dead."

"Maybe 'useful' should be redefined," said Miriam "You're useful in ways you never were before. To your children and your grandchildren, for instance."

"That may be, but I've got to do my work."

Mother talked. Miriam seemed content to let her ramble. She talked about the past: kidskin gloves again and chauffeur-driven cars; Aunt Sylvia, her dearest, oldest friend who had died two weeks ago. "I have a lot of friends and not one except Sylvia knows a thing about me," she said proudly. "Only Sylvia . . . and now she's dead."

Miriam asked Joel how he thought my mother seemed. He said she seemed the same as always: a little bit confused. "But you've changed in other ways," he said to Mom. "You're almost noble now."

"The kids won't be here next week," Mother said to Miriam as we were leaving. "They're going waterskiing in Vermont."

"Cross-country, Mother," I corrected through my teeth.

"Water, cross-country, what's the difference?" She laughed. It was February.

"Why so early?" I asked when the phone rang two days later. "Is something wrong?"

"I just called to say hello," Mother said.

It was seven-thirty in the morning.

"Oh . . . I didn't know. . . ."

Vermont was days and nights of icy, biting cold, of Mother always on my mind, of calling home each night.

"She feels rotten," Daddy said. "The doctor did a liver scan today."

Despite it all, I had a good vacation. It was clear as the New England air how much healing there is in a change of scene. No matter what was in my head, my surroundings were different and that helped.

70

"The scan's okay," my father said the next night. "But she's still feeling lousy."

The distance made my father's plight seem harder than my mother's. She got attention, sympathy, commiseration. She was the patient, after all. But all he had were pressures and her constant presence. He was the one who ought to get away. Joel and I decided we would encourage him to take some time off.

My diary for February 7: *Home. Daddy says it's all downhill with Mother, but it's not and that's the problem. I don't want her dead. I just want this over with. I want to have more fun.*

Fun. I cringed while writing that. As if to be aware of it would make the thought a little less grotesque. But—God forgive me—wanting fun was part of what I felt.

I felt revulsion, too, at my euphemistic side.

"I just want this over with," I wrote, and shook to see that "over with" meant I wanted Mother dead.

I was some lovely child.

That night my father's voice was strained. "What's wrong?" I said.

"Mother spent two hours in the kitchen fixing what I thought was soup and eggs for dinner. She just called me in to eat."

The panic in his voice was palpable.

"On my plate were meatballs and spaghetti. Frozen stiff."

He paused.

"Something is very wrong," he said. "Something is very wrong with her, I mean."

I could almost hear his throbbing forehead vein.

"We have to do something."

"I'll be right down," I said. "But let me talk to Mother for a minute."

"I'm okay now," she said. She sounded very strong. "I

71

must have had a little lapse. But I'm okay. Don't worry."

She said she didn't know she hadn't heated Daddy's dinner, but now she did and now she was all right. "I'm fine. Please don't come down. As soon as I'm done with dinner, I want to go to bed."

I said I'd be there in the morning.

Next morning Mother called at nine.

"I'm fine," she said. "Don't worry."

February 8 - March 2

Don't worry.

The bedroom blinds were shut tightly, the curtains drawn—at noon.

"Hi, Mom," I said.

I flipped the switch. A sea of rags appeared.

"What's going on?" I asked.

No answer.

"Mom—"

The room looked like a mill ends shop; shreds of former sheets lay on the floor, toweling on the tabletop, the chair . . .

I neared the bed. A piece of light blue terry-cloth was covering her eyes!

"Mother!" I was shaking her. "What the hell is happening? Why do you have a rag on your face?" My throat was tight, my voice a high-pitched whine.

"It keeps the sun away," she said. "I can't find my other rag. This one will do as well."

The air was thick and heavy. I couldn't catch my breath.

"I'm opening a window, Mom. It stinks of cigarettes in here."

"No, don't. I like the smell of smoke. I like the smell of lemons, too."

Long ago I read that every child taking care of ailing parents will—if the illness goes on for long enough—run smack into the wall of What Can't Be Stood Another Moment and confront what makes an institution thinkable. For almost everyone, the author said, the limit is incontinence. Children who can tolerate nearly anything, he wrote, can rarely stand to see their parents soiling themselves.

I always knew—for me—withdrawal would be worse.

I remember Mother in the middle of a fight, the way she'd turn to ice, unplug, shut down. And I remember how the lockout was a punishment far worse for me than spankings, threats, or screams, how lack of access always felt like death.

And there she lies: a slab with rag accompaniment.

"Oh, Mom."

I throw myself beside her. "I'm so scared."

"I'm fine," she says.

She isn't there.

I lie on her unbreasted side. She pats my head, and then the bed, and then my head.

I cry.

"Come back to me. I'm terrified."

"I'm fine," she says.

She isn't mine. She is the wire and terry-cloth mother substitute they use in psychological experiments.

"I'll be all right," she drones.

She is a monkey momma made of rags; her funny mouth makes crazy sounds.

"I swear to God, I'm fine."

"You poor people," Dr. Daniels said between my sobs. "You poor, exhausted people. You haven't had two consecutive good days since September."

So what if he was overbooked and busy? So what if I had spent six minutes waiting on the phone? When, at last, he talked to me he was Hippocrates and Freud: he pitied me. I loved him.

"I know it's hard to wait, but there's not a thing that we can do for your mother over the weekend. And it's too late to take any tests today. So bring her to the office first thing Monday morning."

"Mother is still asleep," my father said at ten the following morning.

At eleven he called back.

"She just asked me if she'd had her coffee yet. And the half-filled cup was sitting right in front of her."

How can I leave a man who's stroke-prone with someone who is slowly going mad? How can I keep those weird and creepy things from crawling through her head? How can I stop my inner screams? Anything but a madwoman for a mother, please. . . .

I packed a bag and raced to their place vowing I would stay until Monday morning. Mother made me leave at three o'clock.

"Sit down and keep me company," she said when I arrived. "I only have a few things left to iron."

She hummed, happy to be doing something useful. She talked—with total clarity—of the plans in progress for her sister Yetta's birthday:

". . . so we're thinking of a luncheon at the Frog. Or do you think the Fairmont might be nicer?"

"I think you've been an inspiration these past months," I said.

She looked at me as if to say, "I thought *I* was the one with mental troubles."

"Come into my room," she said. "I want to watch the basketball game. I need to get my mind off myself."

She stretched out on the double bed, ready to forget herself a blessed little while. She rooted for the team in white, and in between her hearty cheers I provided nonstop play-by-play pronouncements on every change in our relationship since the crises of the previous September.

"Isn't it terrific that we've finally gotten close?"

She nodded absentmindedly and shouted at the television set: "Come on! You only need one point to take the lead."

"I love you, Mom," I said three times in the first quarter.

"I love you, too. But can we talk about it later?"

Later?

Who could count on later? Mother might be out of it or gone from me and it would be too late to make sure *everything* I had inside my heart was said.

"I love you, Mom."

"Me, too. But please . . . let's talk about it later."

"Look, dear," she said finally. "I appreciate your being here, but it's really not necessary. In fact, if you don't mind, I'd like to be alone a little while."

"You're sure?"

"Yes. You see, I *know* I'm having lapses, but in between them I'm the same as usual. I think, perhaps, I'm even clearer than I've been. So I want to try to rest my mind and then I want to figure out what's happening. But I want you to know I think you've been wonderful to me. I'm very grateful."

"I love you, Mom."

"But try to understand. I *have* to try to figure out what's going on."

Luckily she didn't ask for my opinion, for I *knew* the cancer had spread to her brain. I didn't have a doubt about the outcome.

The doctor disagreed.

"There isn't any sign of tumor spread," he said on Monday morning.

But he hadn't seen her when I picked her up: blue shoes, a brown striped blouse, a purple plaid skirt.

And he hadn't heard her answer when I asked what papers I should bring for her to read while we were waiting in his office.

"Bring as many as you can," she said with sad eyes scanning stacks of *Inquirer*s and *Bulletin*s she had saved. "I need to know about everything . . . now."

"There are, however, many signs of stress," he added. "I think depression is a factor here, too. And probably some atherosclerosis. Any or all of which might easily account for your mother's troublesome behavior."

"A physician friend said Prednisone could cause this kind of mental change," I said.

"Perhaps. But I doubt it. I think your mother has had a great deal to face in the past few months. I think she is worried and needs some time alone to think things through."

She nodded.

"I want to increase her dose of Elavil and I'd like *you* to try to see to it that your mother gets some rest . . . some time to herself . . . and that no one pushes her for a little while. Including *you,* Mildred. Take it easy on yourself a little while. You don't have to prove yourself all the time."

"You're right," said Mother. "I *am* depressed. Why shouldn't I be? And I do need to be alone. I'm so worried about Sy. So worried about myself. . ."

"She's under stress," the doctor said. "It's normal. It will pass."

I knew it wasn't normal. I knew this new, peculiar phase was either due to a tumor or to Mother's going through the semi-final stage. If brain metastases were not the cause of discon-

77

nection, then the lapses were rehearsals for her ultimate leave-taking.

I absolutely *knew* it, no matter what the doctor said.

The hell with time alone; I wouldn't leave her side.

Day in and out at Mom's. She sleeps. Wakes in a stupor. Slowly stirs and moves exactly like the pachyderm she's coming to resemble. She is so slow . . . so swollen . . . so full of what she needs . . . and wants . . . and has to have. . . .

"She's normal," Alice told me. "I learned last night that Mother is just like everyone with cancer."

Last night's group was "Families of Cancer Patients."

"You should have heard them," Alice said. "They all said *everyone* with cancer gets self-centered and greedy. They say it's just a phase, though. It will pass."

Meantime . . .

"She asked me to leave work and bring her pea soup yesterday," my sister whispered in the kitchen.

"That's nothing. She asked Ann Eisenbaum to get clam chowder, snapper soup, and crab cakes from Bookbinders."

"Did Annie do it?"

"Of course. And when she dropped the packages off this afternoon, she wouldn't let us pay."

Thinking that the old rules still prevailed, Alice said, "Mother must have been humiliated."

I shook my head. "Not a bit. She just said thanks and went into her room. But Daddy was embarrassed. And *I* wanted to die."

I.

Again.

Still.

Always.

She wanted: Bassetts ice cream, chocolate pudding, chocolate-covered nuts from Shane's; special soups; bread from Le Fournil. She wanted *everything.*

"Guess who *Philadelphia* magazine says has the best cinnamon buns in the city?" she said as we were leaving chemotherapy.

I knew.

"Would you run in and get me some? I'll wait in the car."

"I can't *run* into the Gallery, Mom. Market Street's a mess."

"Tell them that your mother's sick."

"Tell *whom?* Besides, there isn't even any place to *stop*. I can't. Not now. I won't."

"Okay," she said. "No problem. I'll get another stooge to do it."

It's normal, Alice tells me. It will pass.

My father said he wouldn't go away.

"Mother is much too sick," he said. "She shouldn't be alone. And how could I relax when I'm so worried?"

Alice and I, because of *our* needs, urged him to go.

"We're worried about you, too, Daddy. What'll we do if you get sick again? Mother says she wants you to go. She says she needs some time alone. And Dr. Daniels says it's fine. . . ."

Aunt Ethel very graciously said she would come in from New York and stay with Mother for the time he was gone.

"Okay. I'll go," he said at last. "But you must call me every night and promise not to keep a thing from me."

From the moment he agreed to go to Florida my father bloomed: he had more pep; his walk was lighter, his face less gray. He seemed to need less nitroglycerine.

Naturally. There was something to look forward to—something more compelling than a cardiogram.

Unlike me, he had a plan. Except for therapies—chemical two times a month and family each Saturday at noon—I wouldn't book ahead.

Which is not to say I had no social life. My diary, in fact, reminds me there were times I went to dinner, saw a film, or just spent a recharging evening with friends. But none of it

79

was planned. I would shield myself with caveats and warn my friends: "Don't count on me . . . perhaps . . . it all depends."

I lived the way the sages of the East suggest: one day at a time.

It is vastly overrated.

Living only in the now is fine for newts or snakes or cows, but not for people. Humans have to have tomorrows, too.

I started picking fights.

Rich had his chronic winter cough and cold.

"Did you take your vitamin C?" I asked him constantly. "Take it. Try to drink more orange juice. If you give a cold to me, I could pass it on to Nanny. *She* could die."

I mothered Bill with equal sensitivity.

He called from school, sounding low. Everything was cold and gray he said; he had a research paper due and was feeling overwhelmed.

"What are you writing about?" I asked.

"The Crusade movement in northern France from 1096 to 1204. I feel as if I don't know where to start."

"Maybe you should change your major," I advised. "There's not much of a market for medievalists."

He hung up very quickly.

I planned a family night to compensate for all the time I wasn't home. It was to be a date we couldn't break; a time for touching base; a place to air complaints; a way of smoothing out feelings and being close. But my husband and son were not enthusiastic about my family psychic health checks, especially during wrestling season.

Joel, a onetime college wrestler and an all-time grappling fan, and Rich—trying for a spot on varsity—wanted to talk "scissors," "whizzers," "switches," "Granby's," "drags," and "locks"; I wanted to talk needs. They spoke of rolls, reverses, rides, and moves. I was interested in moods. *My* areas of expertise—Feelings and Terminal Disease—had

80

nothing to do with falls or making weight, so no one talked to me. Invariably I steamed and ended up resorting to the one technique that always got me into family talks I felt left out of: criticism.

"Use your napkin. Eat your meat. Be quiet when your mouth is full of food," I'd say to Rich.

To Joel I'd drop subtle hints about how difficult it was for me to be so utterly alone with so much grief and how if I *only* had someone who cared at home. . .

A bit of bitchiness, another fight. *Anything* to get connected.

"You're getting morbid," Joel said one night when I had turned away from him. Again. "All you think about and read about and talk about is death."

"What should I be doing? A soft-shoe?"

"I think you ought to try to put it in perspective. Your mother isn't on the critical list. And you don't *have* to be there every minute. Your father said he wants to do more—especially before he goes away. And next week Ethel's coming. You could let your sister help more, too. We need to do some living of our own. Let's go out to dinner Friday night."

"I'll have to see how Mother is. I can't make any plans."

Except to get to Death and Dying class.

The first class was scheduled for Tuesday, February 27.

"Please don't sit in rows," says the smiling, dark-haired woman standing at the door.

I know what's coming: a move into encounter shape.

"Form a semicircle."

I am right.

"Please say your name. Then use three adjectives beginning with your first initial to describe yourself to us."

I hate these gimmicky ways of making people open up to one another. I should have known and not sat on an end. Then I wouldn't have to be the first to speak. I wish my

81

name were Cynthia or Sue. Everything that starts with "D" is dumb.

"And then please share with us the reasons that you took this class."

Oh well.

"I am Diane. I am desolate about my parents. My husband says I'm death-obsessed. Maybe I'm depressed. I used to be delightful."

A dear friend sits next to me. She is joyous (her year of chemotherapy just ended); sometimes jealous (of women with two breasts); occasionally jumpy. She is Jackie.

Two seats away from her an honest, hateful, heavy-hearted soul; and next to *her* a tender person, terrified, and trapped. Farther down, an "F" who overflows: "I'm fat and frank," she says; "flighty, frightened, and fearful; I'm a failure. I'm fatigued. . . ."

The leader shuts her up

"Thanks for sharing that," she says. And, turning to her neighbor, "You?"

The neighbor is scared, serious, and shaken.

Such harsh, judgmental parts of speech we fifteen women choose! The odds are excellent that more than one of us is *sometimes* simultaneously happy, generous, and kind. But one would not get that impression after hearing *us* present our guilty cases. *Everyone* evaluates herself a minimum of two times nastier than nice. Is that a consequence of how we feel about ourselves around the death, the dying, or the loss we've come to talk about?

There is a bibliography. I am surprised to see some recommended books I haven't read. We learn the names of agencies to will our bodies to. Old stuff for me. We are told to keep a journal and to write reactions to the death and dying topics we talk about in class. Our homework is passed around: an "Attitude Toward Death" test we are to take and bring to class next week at which time we will share our attitudes toward death with everyone.

It should be a snap for me.

I'm scared.

How long before he turns to someone who won't turn away or be asleep or cry when he comes near?

Not only did I fear I would lose my husband to somebody sexier, I worried that a part of me I used to like and liked to use was permanently gone. Desire had disappeared. I was entirely uninterested in sex except as something that, perhaps, I ought to do in order not to lose my man, or an activity I should pursue to get a good night's sleep.

I tried last night. I thought I even wanted to make love. But when I closed my eyes I saw my mother's face and felt her rubbery, unnatural flesh—as if she were embalmed. I couldn't do it.

"I can't," I sobbed. "I'm sorry. But I can't."

He's right. I'm getting morbid.

She cracked two eggs into a yellow Pyrex bowl and shook some salt and pepper in; she added milk, took her fork . . . and stared.

What now? she thought.

My father's face was red. "I had to show her how to scramble *eggs*," he said to me that afternoon. "All she did was stare at them."

"I was stumped," said Mom. "I didn't know what I was doing, but I did it by myself just now to prove that I could conquer it."

No.

"I put the pot roast in the dishwasher just now. I wonder why. For a minute I forgot where it belonged . . . but finally I got it right."

No. No.

"You kids have been terrific," said Aunt Yetta, Mother's younger sister. "Uncle Harry and I would like to take you both to dinner and a movie Thursday night to show you our appreciation."

I didn't want to go. If not on duty, I preferred to be at home where I could read about intractable pain or try to get some sleep.

"I can't," I said. "But thanks."

"Do me a favor," Mother said next morning. "It means a lot to Yetta to take you and Alice out. Please let her do it. It would mean a lot to me."

We go.

"Would you like a cocktail?" Yetta says. "I hear the lobster is excellent. I'll have the steak, but please have anything you want. Would you like some wine?"

God knows they're being gracious, trying to entertain. They talk politics, history, and books on the best-seller list.

I yawn.

I hope they think I'm overworked and tired. They must not know I'm bored, that this is not intense enough for me.

I don't belong in public anymore. I don't belong with company. I hate: my sister's skirt; Aunt Yetta's yellow sweater; the fuss that Harry is making over me.

We leave the restaurant and walk two blocks through icy winds. I'm miserable, but we must see the preview of the film everyone is up in arms about: *The Deer Hunter*.

The lights dim; the curtains part. There on a giant screen a world of blood and gore unfolds, a universe of grief and agony, a hell.

I feel right at home.

"Thank you for a perfect night," I say as we depart. "The movie was precisely what I needed."

They think I am kidding. They think I'm being flip, but they're wrong.

It's Joel who is right.

I've grown morbid to my core.

"Diane looks a little like her sister," said the lady who was polishing Mom's nails.

"She doesn't have a sister," Mother said.

The manicurist looked at me. My mother saw. "Oh," she sighed, "it's *that* Diane. Of course. I had forgotten. . . ."

Daddy goes tomorrow. If he goes. He's scared to death to leave her. Who can blame him?

Dinner is fixed. They bicker. I guess for him to go they must not feel too close. It sounds a lot like old times, though. I wish they wouldn't fight.

She sleeps so much. And when she's up she eats, enumerates her needs, and rarely asks about the kids . . . the cat . . . my life.

No matter.

I no longer have a life but this.

At Miriam's, the morning Daddy left, Alice reports:

"I dropped Daddy at the airport at nine-thirty this morning. He's uneasy about being away from Mother. But it's *only* for ten days."

"He's worried," Miriam said. "He cares a lot about her."

Mother's fat and waxy face was beaming.

"Something beautiful happened last night," she announced.

At two in the morning, when neither one of them could sleep, they sat together in the kitchen.

"He kept saying how he loved me, how he wanted me to know he always had, how even though there'd been a lot of bad times, in the time that we had left we ought to try to make it good. . . ."

"Daddy talked like *that?*" we asked in chorus.

Mother nodded.

Miriam smiled.

"This family. . ." she said.

"This family has been wonderful," said Mother. "It's very hard for me. I'm weak. And now I have these times when I don't know what I'm doing. But you kids have been so

85

good . . . and Sy . . . so kind to me. And his sisters . . . wonderful. Mine, too. I'm so grateful. And I'm fighting like hell. I want to beat this thing."

"You're very brave," said Miriam.

"I try. I don't want to be a burden. And I don't *ever* want to lose my dignity."

"You never will, Mildred. You're entirely a lady. You will always have your dignity."

Mother grew six inches.

"This family. . ." said Miriam again.

Mother interrupted. "I heard Sy and Alice disagree about something the other night. I don't know what it was. It doesn't matter. What matters is that they didn't get into a nasty argument. They didn't yell. They talked. It felt so good to me."

"That's terrific!" Miriam said. "Alice, aren't you pleased? Your mother is really glad you're growing up."

"I guess," said Alice.

Miriam turned to me.

"How do *you* feel about it? Do you think that you can stand to see your sister change? It will certainly shift *your* role in the family if Alice is a grown-up, too."

"Of course I can," I answered glibly. "It's what I've always wanted."

"This family," said Miriam, "is doing a really fine piece of work."

That afternoon I wrote:

Let go, let go, let go.

I love you, Mom. I no longer need to spend my time denying there's a Mildred part of me.

You do have dignity.

You are a lady.

Brave and strong.

You've set me a magnificent example.

But you've done it long enough. Enough. I'm done. Oh,

Mom. I'm so tired of your pain. So worn out from the worry.
So please . . . let go.

Some fine daughter I turned out to be.

Ethel's telephone hello is the aural equivalent of hugs and
lilies of the valley. She used to have a television show.

"Hello."

Must she sound so goddamned cheery?

"How is Mom this morning?"

"She's running the water for her bath and laying out her
clothes. We're going out to lunch with Emily and Bea."

How come she's going out with you? The only place she
ever goes with *me* is to the doctor.

"Yes, but, how does she feel?"

"Hold on. I'll see if she can speak to you."

You'll see? How dare you ask my mother if she wants to
speak to *me?*

"Please, Aunt Ethel, put her on the phone."

My father's voice, long distance, was relaxed.

"I slept for nine hours straight," he announced. "For the
first time since September. And I walked on the beach after
dinner. Tomorrow I'm planning to play golf. Now tell me
about Mother."

Headaches, Daddy. Aspirin. But nothing worse, I swear.
The same old in and out of knowing what she's doing. Nothing new.

"She's sleeping," Ethel says.

"She's been asleep for four hours. Wake her up," comes
my command.

"I don't think. . ."

"Please wake her up, Aunt Ethel. Otherwise she'll be
awake all night."

"I guess you're right. Last night she was writing checks at

two o'clock and sealing them in envelopes without addresses."

Aspirin, Daddy. Ice bags. And some signs that bother me. An ice-cream stain on her sheet she either didn't see or didn't care about. A spot of something on a spoon she hadn't gotten clean. But Ethel helps her dress and gets her out for lunch or dinner every single day which is more than you or I could ever do.

"She's vomiting," says Ethel. "She says her head hurts horribly."
"I'll be right down."
"No need. I'm managing."
Exactly. That's the problem.
"She's looking for her credit cards. She can't remember where they are. When she finds them you should hide them."

Someone listen. Something's wrong. She didn't take her pills last night. And this morning when I told her I'd be down at ten she said, "You better get here earlier. It's important that you have your tea on time."

"A brain scan," Dr. Daniels said. "As soon as possible. I don't like the look of things."
A brain scan. Friday afternoon at one o'clock.

"Your mother was magnificent at dinner last night," Aunt Bea said. "Her attitude is amazing. And her strength, her steeliness. Such a change in her whole personality."
"Did she make sense?" I was ashamed to ask; afraid not to.
"Absolutely. She was quieter than usual, but when she spoke she made perfect sense."

I almost wish she would be crazy constantly just to show I'm not imagining this nightmare.

"No, dear. The brain scan isn't until one," I say. "But I'll be down before eleven."

I must get the credit cards and take away her checkbook. Ethel says she's signing checks and leaving open the amounts.

"No, dear. Lunch with Ruth is *after* therapy on Saturday. *Tonight* Aunt Yetta's having you and Ethel to her house for dinner."

She's lying on the bed.

"Hi, Mom." I kiss her cheek.

"I hope it is a nine and not a one with seven C," she says to me. "It was a seven, three, and five they gave to Sylvia."

"What?"

"A nine and not a seven C."

"What are you *talking* about?"

I am beside her. Crying.

"I don't want you worrying and crying. Don't worry. If I'm dying and I'm this confused I won't even know it. You are young. You should have fun."

"I'm not so young. And I'll always manage to have fun. I like to play. . ."

"I play, too. I'd like to play a four, five, seven now."

My God! My mother talks in tongues.

March 2 - March 12

"I'm sorry, but you'll have to wait," the secretary said. "We're running late because of three emergencies. You'll have to wait at least an hour for the scan. I'm really very sorry, but. . ."

I shrugged.

What else was new?

Life is like obedience school when you're a patient or a patient's ombudsman: the task you must continually master is to sit . . . to stay . . . to wait.

You wait until you're fitted into "doctor's very busy schedule" and you wait—without complaint—until it's your turn. You wait until you're tested, typed, injected; wait for X-rays to be taken and for X-rays to be read and for word that "you may leave now, they're okay." You wait for dye to circulate, for dye to be absorbed. You wait for diagnoses and for options and for odds. You wait to ask your questions, and when you forget one, you phone it in and then wait hours at home until you're called back.

You wait . . . you sit . . . you stay. . . .

"I'm really very sorry. . ."

So we had another wait.

What else was new?

I shrugged.

I settled Mother on a vinyl-covered love seat, gave the secretary Medicare and Blue Cross information, and hurried out to move the car I had parked illegally on Eighth Street.

A meter maid was tucking in my punishment.

"Please," I grabbed the ticket and waved it in her face. "Can't you tear this up? I've only been five minutes. I had to help my mother in . . ."

"I'm sorry, lady. There's the sign. It says 'No Stopping.' "

"Yes, I know, I see. But it was *only* for a minute. She has to have a brain scan. She is very sick."

"Sorry, but there's nothing I can do. You're not supposed to stop here."

"But my mother has cancer . . . she . . ."

"Look, lady, I'm just doin' my job."

"Christ, lady! So am I."

"Did you get a ticket?" Mother said.

"No," I lied.

"Good. Maybe that's an omen."

I used the time to tell her why I had to take her credit cards away.

"I know," she said. "Don't worry."

"I'll seal them in an envelope in front of you and I'll give them to Daddy as soon as he gets back."

"You don't have to go to such extremes. I trust you. And don't worry."

"But I want to take your checkbook from you, too."

"That's okay. You'd better. I guess I'm dangerous when I don't know what I'm doing."

She left me for a second—mentally.

"It's hell to *know* you don't know what you're doing," she announced on her return.

91

The waiting area for brain scan candidates at Pennsylvania Hospital is simultaneously a front-row seat and stage. The space—twelve paces by fifteen—is directly to the right of the main entrance of the Spruce Street building. It has no door, no screen for privacy, just a sofa and a love seat backed against the barren walls where patients and their people sit, where all the traffic has to pass, where every passerby can see.

While Mother dozed, I made some intermittent notes and watched the people watch me watching them.

Visitors sped toward the elevators in the rear; three denim-covered men lugged giant loads of laundry through the doors. Doctors who had been on one case or another of one parent or the other hurried past; some nodded; several smiled. I recognized some nurses, too. Cleaning men and women tended to the shiny vinyl floor and orderlies went by, diligently indifferent to the matchstick men and women in the wheelchairs they were pushing.

Please, God, I prayed, do not let it be that what I see is what my mother gets.

"Mildred Rubin, please."

A weary nurse recited the instructions: "You will have to lie perfectly still, Mildred. The doctor will inject a dye into your arm. Then you might feel hot all over for a moment. Or you may just feel strange in the back of your throat. Or even slightly nauseated."

"That's no problem," Mother said. "That's exactly how I'm feeling all the time these days."

"Fine," responded Florence Nightingale. "Now sign right here before we start."

"Why?" I wanted to know.

"Because of the dye."

"Oh."

You get tired. Sometimes knowing doesn't matter half as much as getting on with it. And if the nurse had listed all the bad things that the dye might do, what then?

I signed for Mother. And I said, "Can I stay with her while you are doing it?"

"No. You have to sit outside. Take her handbag and her wig and wait. Just stay out there. She'll be done in half an hour. You can wait outside the door."

Arf. Arf.

On the love seat, next to me, is Mother's pocketbook and the Bonwit Teller shopping bag that's stuffed with all the newspapers Mother carries everywhere and doesn't read. Her frosted wig sits on my lap. I close my eyes and see a small, bald head moving through the hole of the machine in the gray room behind the door I left her in alone.

I cannot stand it.

My eyes come open, spot the wig. I start to cry.

I cry for tiredness and pain, for what makes people shrink, for being bald, for loss and fear, for Mom, for Pop.

For me.

I think I'm feeling sorry for myself.

I'm crying harder, now.

The passing people look at me and quickly look away. Not only that, the sight of me accelerates their pace.

I know, I know . . . A woman on a love seat by herself with a wig on her lap looks weird.

But doesn't anyone feel moved to offer something?

With all the people going by, doesn't *someone* want to know if he . . . or she . . . can help?

Guess not.

Would I?

Who knows.

It's awkward to go up to someone you don't know and say, "What's wrong?"

You might be told.

The gods in charge of empathy took charge of me that wretched second day of March. As I waited, so miserable and raw, for my mother's scan, I visualized a hundred

93

thousand other scared and weary middle-aged people who waited, too; who cried—inside or out—and wanted just as much as I to do the right and loving thing for their sick folks, but often couldn't, for they hadn't half as much to cushion them as I. If I, with health and love and money for my every need and many of my wants, with family and friends to give support, with stamina, access to and knowledge of the system and the shortcuts and the ways to grease the wheels, could find it so impossible to cope, what about the others with so much less?

How do you do it when you aren't well yourself? When you can't afford the loss of pay the day away from work entails? How do you stand it when you have to wait on cold, windy corners for a bus that doesn't come and someone very dear and very sick is leaning on an aching arm? What do you do when your mate resents your time away? Or when nobody cares at all?

Life has to be a constant open sore.

The only helpful thing I thought of was a corps of gentle volunteers who might be stationed at the places in a hospital where all the people who attend the seriously ill are always parked: cardiac care; intensive care; dialysis departments; nuclear medicine. The volunteers could do the simple tender things: go for tea; offer tissues; listen.

Such attention might provide the only kindness some poor tired souls might know.

"This is the end, I know it," Mother told me as I drove her home.

"I don't know if that's true," I lied.

"I hurt."

"Where?"

"Under my heart . . . in the middle of my belly. And I'm so awfully tired."

"I love you, Mom," I said and rubbed her hand. "We *all* love you a lot."

"I know. And that's what makes it harder."

94

Once home she turned to counting buttons on her house-coat. She had to know how many towels she owned. She asked, "How many prenisons again?" And said, "Please turn the water down to eight and remember to ask Joel to fix seven."

Numbers, Daddy, numbers.

"You're telling me? Two nights ago she called to say that I should bet a four, five, seven combination at the racetrack. She was sure it would come in, she said. Well, I went last night and bet it."

"How'd you do?"

"I won four hundred dollars. . . . I'm too worried to stay away. I'm coming home tomorrow afternoon."

On Saturday, March 3, we were scheduled to see Miriam at eleven. Alice planned to pick up Mother at ten-thirty. I would meet them at Miriam's.

Ethel's first call came at 9:00 A.M.

"Mother wants to go downstairs and wait for Alice *now*," she said.

"That's crazy. Let me talk to her."

"Hello."

The voice was wrong.

"Mom, are you okay? Do you know who this is?"

"I guess."

If she knew, she didn't care.

"Put Ethel on again."

"Do anything," I said to Ethel, "but please be sure she's in the lobby at ten-thirty. It's important that some other people see her in this state."

Mother, knowing that she sometimes spoke in code, had grown slyly quieter with those not very close.

"I'll do my best," Aunt Ethel said.

Call two arrived at ten.

"Mother says she *has* to go downstairs now, so I am going with her."

"But Alice isn't due for half an hour."

"I know. But she insists that she is going now. And I can't let her go alone."

At ten-fifteen, again:

"Hello?"

"Diane, dear," Aunt Ethel sang. "Alice isn't here yet."

Good God. Was Mother's craziness contagious?

"Are *you* going crazy, too?" I yelled. "You know damn well that Alice isn't due until ten-thirty."

"Don't take that tone with me. . . ."

"Don't tell me how to talk. . . ."

Aunt Ethel had taken a week away from work—a week she called vacation—and come to Philadelphia to take constant loving care of Mother. For that she got a stab at cracking Mother's esoteric number code; a chance to practice keeping ice bags filled; and endless opportunities to fetch the hundred things my mother wanted "desperately" and right away.

She also got my barely hidden jealousy and, finally, my sass.

So absorbed was I with my own misery, I forgot I wasn't all alone in hell.

Someone should have slapped my thoughtless mouth.

Alice ambled into Miriam's alone.

"I got there at ten-thirty," she said to Miriam and me, "but Mother wasn't in the lobby. So I double-parked and called up to her apartment from the desk. Ethel said that Mother couldn't come. She was too tired."

I coiled. "You didn't even try to talk her into it?"

"No. Why should I? If she's too tired, why should she be forced to come?"

I tried explaining what had gone before . . . all morning . . . but the effort was too much. My voice was much too tight.

"Don't talk like that to me," my sister said. "And while

we're at it—since it's only *us*—why don't we talk to Miriam about the way you *usually* speak to me?"

"I think that is a fine idea," said Miriam.

Not me.

"I don't want to deal with *you* right now," I said to Alice and I turned to Miriam. "I've got too many other things to think about."

I started listing Mother's symptoms, alluded to my celibate state, mentioned tension, lack of sleep, and a shortening fuse.

Miriam repeated that my sister had a point. Alice, I remember, called me bossy. After that, it's all a blank. Rage, my ever-present tenant, took possession and evicted any trace of rationality.

"You little brat," I burst out at Alice.

That was the high point of a diatribe that lives in memory because it made me feel alive the way *The Deer Hunter* had.

Fury made my juices flow. I don't remember what I said. But without sick parents to be careful of, with Miriam to stave off actual murder, I went berserk. I shouted ugly things I didn't know I still contained and hurled at Alice every anger real and fancied that I had stored for almost forty years.

Alice, of course, tried to interrupt, which so offended me that I indignantly stood up, pronounced my standard exit line: "You don't want me in charge? That's fine! But you'll have to do it by yourself, because I am THROUGH!" and stormed out.

I came home soaking wet.

Joel said I had a message from Aunt Yetta. Aunt Yetta said Aunt Ethel didn't like the way I had spoken to her. Aunt Ethel called to tell me—frostily—that she was calling on behalf of Mom who wanted her to say she hoped that Alice and I did well at Miriam's. Daddy called to tell me he was home. Aunt Ethel called again, at five o'clock, to say she had done the inventory of the freezer and had left it on the counter in the kitchen.

"What inventory?" I said.

"The one that Alice asked me for."

"I don't understand."

"When Alice brought your father home this afternoon, she said she thought she ought to know exactly what was in the freezer. She said too many things were going bad because they weren't being used in time."

"Alice told you *that?*"

"She did, and I've done it. Now, is there anything else you'd like me to do? I'm going home tomorrow morning."

"Ask Alice. She's in charge."

I never would have thought to ask somebody else to do the freezer.

How does Alice know from delegating?

That night I picked a vicious fight with Joel; the next morning I nagged relentlessly at Rich. By Sunday noon Ethel, Alice, Joel, and Rich were my enemies for sure.

By two o'clock I had apologized and cried a lot.

"Poor dear. It is so hard for you . . ." was the consensus.

Everyone is understanding. Everyone forgives.

Not me.

I cannot stand myself like this.

But I'm so tired. So scared.

The brain scan was normal.

"Perhaps the Prednisone *is* to blame. I think it should be stopped," the doctor said. "But keep in close touch. And if her lapses don't get better soon . . . we'll see. Call me if there are any problems."

Problems?

Daddy took a walk and came back red of face and staggering.

"What's wrong?" I ran to him.

"I'm not sure, but I feel funny."

"Your heart?" I asked.

"My head."

I gave him aspirin, took him to his room, and called his doctor.

Bed rest. Tranquilizers. "Be sure to call me if there are any problems," Dr. Binnion said.

Problems?

Daddy slept. I checked on Mom.

"Did you ever hear it called a blessing?" Mother blurted from apparent sleep.

"Hear what?"

"Death."

"Yes."

"Well, when I die I want you to think of it like that. I don't want you to have recriminations. You have all been wonderful and this has been, in many ways, a very fruitful year. Is that clear?"

Before I could respond, she added, "Now, please, give me a five and number three."

"Oh, Mother, what's a five?"

"You know . . . oh . . . am I doing it again?"

"Yes. What's a five?"

"Two twos." We laughed. "Oh, this is maddening. . . ."

"I know. But try not to worry, Mom. You've stopped the Prednisone so . . . maybe soon . . ."

"I hope so. Now could I have the three?"

Back to Daddy.

"You okay?"

"It was just an incident," he said. "Don't worry. I'll be fine in a few hours. But would you hand me my nitroglycerine—quickly—please?"

Worry? Me?

Some parts of Death and Dying class were much like kindergarten, with Show and Tell relabeled Show and Share. We no longer simply spoke, we shared.

"I think that we should share our feelings about the questionnaire."

"I liked it very much," said H.

"Thanks for sharing that."

"I didn't like it. I felt scared."

"I'm glad you shared that, too."

"I've felt guilty ever since my brother suffocated," M. said. She was almost crying.

"Thank you for sharing that."

I didn't like the way "sharing" took the place of saying something straight, nor did I like that it implied a depth of feeling no one ought to criticize. It seemed to me that so much "sharing" conned you into feeling close and thus seduced you out of seeing what your ordinary judgment normally would know was mean or dumb. Baring deepest secrets is no guarantee of intimacy. And every feeling isn't splendid just because it has been announced.

The argot alienated me. I thought it was entirely too slick. I also thought much of the death and dying talk was whistling in the dark. But there *was* a warmth and concern I liked. The leader had a strong commitment to improving conditions for the ill and she laid great stress on listening.

"Don't assume the dying want what *you* think you would want," she said a dozen times. "Ask, and listen. If you don't do anything else, listen, just listen."

She wanted us to fight the isolation of the terminally ill. "Most people—professionals included—avoid the dying. If I don't do another thing, let me convince you to work to see that people facing death are not alone if they don't want to be."

But as far as making death less mysterious or minimizing fear—which is surely why we earnest students came—it didn't help. I came to see the movies and the books, the tapes and television shows, the seminars and workshops, and descriptions of death's stages as serving the same purpose as the pots of water men of bygone generations were routinely sent to boil while their wives were giving birth: something to be doing; busy work.

To talk about dying was not to know death. And though the kidney gifts and living wills and cemetery plots decided on ahead of time were fine because they might improve another's life or be of some small consolation to survivors, they didn't demystify the dying. Death was not a problem we could analyze away. When we had finished sharing, we were still entirely alone.

The burns appeared suddenly: brown circles on the carpet near her bed, holes in the quilt and on three robes.

"You must promise not to smoke unless somebody is in the room with you," I admonished her.

She nodded.

What was I doing asking for her word? What she knew then were fives and nines, not self-discipline.

The bed itself didn't seem quite right: I counted a fitted sheet on the bottom, three flat sheets on top of one another beneath the quilt, and a final, flowered, flat sheet on top of everything.

"Mother, who made the bed like this?" I moaned.

"I did. Is something wrong? Does it need another sheet?"

And there were starting to be public leaks.

"Would you like dessert?" The waitress stopped the cart in front of us.

"I think I'll have a three," said Mom. She pointed to the chocolate cake.

The waitress blinked.

"A what?" she said.

"I've got two threes, I only need one more."

The waitress looked at me.

"Could she have her coffee, please?" I laughed. "And chocolate cake?"

"You know that I'm not making fun of you when I laugh, don't you, Mom?"

"I do. I also know exactly what the numbers mean. What's awful is I can't explain it."

My father asked to talk to me, alone.

"I want you to call Dr. Daniels," he said. "I don't think he's leveling with us. Mother is getting worse. And if the cancer isn't doing this, then maybe the chemicals are destroying her brain cells. Maybe she should stop the chemotherapy."

"I'm sure he's being honest with us, Daddy. But why don't *you* call him if you have some questions?"

That suggestion stunned us both.

My father said he might.

He did.

"He wants her to see a neurologist. A Dr. Cook. Next Monday at noon."

Dr. Cook walked into the waiting room at 11:55:—a man in his early forties, medium height, dark hair parted neatly on the side.

"Mrs. Rubin? I am Dr. Cook."

He shook her hand, Daddy's, mine. He smiled, not rushing. I liked him right away.

"Why don't you follow me into my office? First we'll talk and then I'll examine you."

"Thank you, doctor," Mother said.

He stationed Mother in the armchair to his right, put us opposite his desk, and started with a history. All questions were, at first, addressed to Mother. But she didn't want to talk, so she referred him back to Dad and me.

"She's embarrassed," I explained. "She's afraid she'll talk in numbers, and when she does she's ashamed. Especially in front of strangers."

102

"Tell me about the numbers."

"She uses them in place of nouns and adjectives. They have a logic in each sentence, but they're never used consistently. She knows they don't make sense to anyone but her, but when they come she cannot stop them even though she knows . . ."

"Tell me about the numbers, Mildred," he said softly.

"Well," she said, "they have to do with Cs and eights and fours. C four is not a problem anymore, but I badly need a six."

She laughed.

God bless him, so did he.

"Am I going to get better, Dr. Cook?" she asked.

"Of course," he said.

He led her to a room. "Please get into this gown and I'll come back and examine you."

He made her tap the wall and push his hands and follow tiny lights; she touched the places on her arm that he had pinched.

"Walk forward, Mildred," he ordered. "Good. Now walk back. That's excellent. Now let me see you waddle like a duck."

He squeezed her, stuck her, shoved, and shook. She became increasingly afraid.

"Am I doing everything okay?" she finally asked.

"You're doing fine. Now name the presidents for me. Start with Carter and go backward."

"Carter, Nixon, Kennedy . . . I can't remember after that."

We waited—only briefly—while Cook conferred with Daniels privately on the phone. He beckoned me into his office.

"Dr. Daniels agrees that your mother should be hospitalized for tests. I want to do a spinal tap, an EEG, and maybe other things. Although a scan ruled out metastases to the brain, it didn't look at the spinal fluid," he said.

I winced.

"I know," he said. "But we must rule out everything. Infection could be causing this. Or six months of the Prednisone. We just don't know. I think we should investigate."

"Okay," I said. "I'm certain that Mother will do whatever you recommend. Would you try to see if you can get a private room for her?"

"I'll go," she said when he presented his opinion. "But would you see if I can have a private room?"

"Why were you so quiet in his office, Daddy?"
"What?"
"I said, why so quiet when we were with Dr. Cook?"
"I was having trouble hearing."

Mom and Dad went home to nap. I tried it, too. But when I closed my eyes I saw the tumor swimming stealthily through my mother's spinal fluid. I bolted up.
The hell with naps. I'll just be tired till they die.

March 12 - March 21

"She's in four twenty-two Spruce Building," the woman in Admissions said. "Go out that door and make a left and cross the street."

"We know," my father said.

We knew, we knew.

Room 422 was not prepared: the bed was not made yet, there was no table tray; the bathroom had no towels, waste basket, tissues, or soap; the bedroom had no storage space. A single chair sat before a narrow closet. One drawer was all we found.

The room could not hold three adults if one was not in bed.

"I'll take a walk while you get settled," Daddy said.

Mother sank into the chair, pulled off her wig, and sighed. Another time she would have had housekeeping on the phone, insisted on a better room, or stalked away indignantly.

Not now.

Now she simply closed her eyes and sighed, while I went into action.

The line between courtesy and groveling is very fine. I cross it every time I act as medical representative for my folks. I will do most anything to make things comfortable, including shuffle. I will smile at whoever is in power to make my requests seem less annoying. I make sure they know I understand that they are understaffed and overworked and that I really hate to bother them, but if they could let me have a piece of this or tell me where to find a drop of that ... then, I thank them profusely. And smile.

Within an hour Mother lay in bed with ice beside her in the bucket, extra paper cups and extra Kleenex nearby, four extra bath towels underneath the bathroom sink, and extra soap and hand cream on the shelf. The television set had been connected. The cleaning woman promised to stop back and mop the floor.

I convinced the resident that taking Mother's history was pointless.

"She was here in December," I told him. "And dozens of times before that. Why don't you check her records instead of asking questions that will only add to her frustration and that she's apt to answer incorrectly anyway, since she's so confused?"

"You're right," he said.

I put cool washcloths on her head and rubbed her legs. I asked her what she wanted for tomorrow's meals. I knew *always* to check off extra butter, extra sugar, extra cream—to order extra everything.

My face was stiff from grinning.

An orderly appeared. He parked the wheelchair and tapped the door. "Is Mildred Rubin here? She has to go to X-ray."

I nodded.

He looked at Mom and then at me. "Hasn't she got a hospital gown?"

"Not yet."

"She has to have one. Wait, I'll get one for you. I know where they're kept."

He gave me two. "It's cold down there. Have her wear them both. And here's a blanket you can wrap around her legs." He turned. "I'll wait outside while you get her ready."

I took her nightgown off and wondered where the nurses were. Who would do this if I weren't here? What do people *do* who don't have me?

I helped her into the wheelchair. "Take care of her," I told him.

"You look like *you* need taking care of just as much as she," he said.

I do, but who will do it?

Mother napped and I went out to walk. I bought two magazines in case she felt like reading, some apples for a snack, and a tiny wicker basket filled with baby's breath and roses.

Sometimes I am nice, I thought. Sometimes I am sweet.

I thought about the ritual close of Death and Dying class. Before we left we'd go around our circle sharing everything we'd done to make that particular Tuesday count.

"Telling what you do to make a day count makes you more aware of living well," the leader said. "It also helps you find out what you really value. So now let's share with one another: What did *you* do to make today count?"

Walking back to Mother's room I warmed myself with fantasies of me at center stage that night, dazzling all my Death and Dying mates with details of my utterly devoted day. How they would envy me the chance to do so many last and loving things, I thought. How much they'd wish their day had counted half as much as mine. I saw myself outshining everybody in the class, outdoing anybody in the city, as virtuous as anybody in the world.

107

But with such notions how was I to see myself as either nice or sweet?

Dr. Cook stopped by shortly after I returned. He took his time with Mother, which was a comfort. He said that he suspected subclinical infection. He said the spinal tap was scheduled for tomorrow. He told me I looked tired.

My face was out of shape from so much smiling.

A man with broomstick arms and toothpick legs and tubes connected to a bottle on an intravenous stand talks to the woman sitting next to me.

"Two operations and now this."

I act as if I'm very busy writing, for I do not want to speak. I do not wish to list my patient's symptoms. I don't want entrance to the waiting room fraternity. I, therefore, try to look absorbed.

"I've had two operations and I'm getting chemotherapy," the man says. "But I'm losing too much weight which is why I'm wearing this." He gestures toward the IV bottle and mentions megavitamins.

"My husband is getting radiation," says the lady.

"Oh, I had that. It's not too bad except for sometimes being nauseating."

Their conversation goes round and round, past cancer to the cost of medical care to last night's television shows.

"Did you see Tom Snyder?" says the lady.

"No. I don't have a television set this time. I can't afford it."

Oh, my God. He can't afford a TV set. I do not want my shame to show so I write faster, frantically.

"I try to get a roommate who can share the cost with me," he says. "But sometimes I can't."

To have the television set connected costs $2.70 a day.

I spend almost that on sugarless gum and mints.

I tell my folks about the conversation, knowing what they'll say.

108

"Did you offer to pay for it for him?"

"I didn't know how. I was too embarrassed. I didn't want to embarrass him and I didn't want to make a grandstand play. It was too awkward."

"Find out the number of his room," they say in unison. "And leave word for the television man to stop in here."

This was my parents at their best: the kind and quiet thoughtful act; the generosity that—not to shame—would stay anonymous.

The check picked up—"This one's on me." Or, "Here's a little something that might help."

It was their finest way of being.

Mom lies flat post-spinal tap and dozes. I give her sips of water, answer the telephone, and wait. She lies there heavy-eyed and blinks. She looks as if there's something on her mind that if she could reach it, would solve the problem of confusion. But no. She only moans and shakes her head.

She stirs.

"Would you light a six for me?" she says.

I put a Pall Mall in her mouth and strike a match.

My father comes in late.

"I would have been here sooner, but I had to clean," he says.

The louse. He knows damn well that on Mother's scale of things to be ashamed of, a man who helps with housework is lower than even semiprivate rooms. But he cannot resist the tease.

"I bet my dishes are cleaner than yours," he says to me.

"Oh, please . . ." my mother says.

But he persists. "How much soap do you use in a mid-sized load of laundry?" he asks. "Is it okay to use cold water? I don't want a ring around *my* collar."

Mother answers fast. She wants the conversation done with. But not my pop. He is very proud. "I ironed some handkerchiefs this morning," he says. "And tomorrow I'll vacuum."

"Oh, please," she says. "Oh, please."

The spinal tap is normal and the EEG is normal and another brain scan is normal, too.

Meantime, *ecce mamma:*

"If a C comes up it would be four C's which would be a Comaneci. Four O's and four M's are all you need, you know. And an S. But now I'm not thinking so much about the S."

She laughs, but her laughs are dry and mirthless. She is scared. "I know I sound crazy, but I can't help it."

She looks uneasily around. She hugs herself and rubs her upper arms. I want to calm her down.

"Why don't I teach you how to meditate?" I say. "Maybe it would help a little bit."

"Why not? I'll try anything."

I tell her everything they taught me in T.M. about the way to let the mantra gently come and not to worry when your thoughts fly all around, but just to drift back easily and simply hear the word that is guaranteed to still your inner self. I show her how to sit.

"Now close your eyes," I say, "and listen to the mantra. It's a word that Dr. Herbert Benson recommends. He says it's absolutely neutral and will soothe you. Are you ready? Good. Now listen, Mom . . . the word is One."

"One?" She jumps. "It *can't* be One! One goes to fives and then I'm thinking eights. . . ."

Thus do I secure her inner peace.

"I am definitely not crazy," Mother said on Thursday afternoon.

Dr. Daniels had arranged for a psychiatrist to see her.

"Dr. Feldman talked to me for half an hour and he said I'm certainly not crazy."

"That's not exactly news, Mom. I knew it. So did you."

"He's coming back on Monday. He said he is thinking of recommending psychotropic drugs."

"Drugs, Dr. Daniels?" I asked.

He was saying something about stress again.

"But this is not the way my mother deals with stress," I said. "She screams. She yells. She gets another sickness. Not like this."

"But she's never been as sick as this," he said. He took his time with me.

"It isn't only stress. I know my mother."

"It isn't only anything, Diane. It's a combination of events, many of which we don't know anything about."

Surprisingly, I didn't mind his ignorance. I thought not knowing kept alive the possibility of change, whereas the label "stress" implied a permanence I hated. Stress and Mother were inseparable. My mother's stress would *never* stop.

"I think she's talking better than five days ago," he said on closing. "Maybe being off the Prednisone will ultimately do the trick. We'll have to wait and see."

But what were we to do in the meantime? She couldn't care for things at home; she was too scared, too weak. It would be much too hard for Daddy, and besides she'd rather die than have him try to care for her.

Should she come to live with us?

"They're not sure why you are talking numbers, Mother, but they think it's probably a combination of stress and Prednisone. They think the longer you are off the drug and the more you can relax, the better the chances are your head will right itself."

"What should I do?"

"Do you want to come to my house until you're clearer and more confident?"

"Yes."

"Are you sure you want to answer quite so fast? Don't you think—just for appearances—you ought to hem and haw a little bit?"

We laugh. If nothing else, there is, at last, an openness between us.

"I think it will be easier for you if I am at your house," she said. "I don't feel as if I'm interfering. I'll go back to my place as soon as I can do my work."

I knew my love of running things could get me into trouble, so I checked with Miriam.

"Do you think I'm right to bring Mother back to stay with me?"

"Will it really be easier for you?"

"Much. I'll only have to cook one set of meals. I won't have to do the driving back and forth."

"Then do it. I don't think your mother is malingering. I'm sure that once she feels stronger she will want to go home."

"But what should I do about my father? I don't want to tell him what to do. And I don't want to come between them, but I think he would be more comfortable at his place."

"Ask him what he wants. Then listen. He will tell you how he feels and what he wants. Just listen."

He didn't want to stay at my house, but was happy, for a week or two, to come out to the suburbs every day and be with Mom. If—and only if—I abided by his terms.

"You must hire someone to help you with Mother, and we'll plan to bring whomever you hire home with us. No matter what your mother says, we have to bring in some-body. You can't keep doing this. And you must let me pay for help and for our share of the food."

I tell Rich that Mother is coming. "It will inconvenience you and I will need some extra help," I say.

112

He answers, "Fine. She'll probably drive me crazy with the cat again, but so what? I love her. I don't mind."

Billy telephones. "Is everything okay? I called the hospital and got no answer. Is everything all right with Nan?"

Joel calls my folks to tell them not to think that they are interfering with our lives or upsetting anything because it really *will* be easier for me to have Mom here.

I know he thinks that if his mother ailed I'd do the same for her and he is right. But my mother-in-law Diana is eighty-three, a busy, healthy, independent woman whom the gods of gerontology created just to show me that there is another side to aging.

She is beautiful and strong, clear of head, and big of heart, my other mother. She has an iron spine. She buses back and forth to work four days a week to "keep from being bored to death."

She will die quietly and fast, I'm sure, at ninety-eight. And then I'll *never* get to pay my sainted husband back.

All that I can do is keep on thanking him.

But I don't sleep. I toss and turn and try to read but can't do more than flip through Kübler-Ross.

Dear Ina called to ask how things were going.

I garbled something, barely coherent.

"You sound very strange," she said. "What's wrong?"

How to answer such a question? I said that I was busy.

"You sound funny. Is something going on? What's wrong?"

What's wrong?

I try a clever quip; my whine comes tumbling out. I say that someone's at the door, "Let me call you back."

What's wrong?

My mother wants to know if I will stop and get three threes for her tomorrow morning. My father did not hear the telephone when I tried to reach him earlier. I was sure he had had another stroke.

I have been a slave for six long months.

Does anyone know how hard this is to do?

I used to read and now I can barely scan the headlines. Anything else is too much of an effort.

Once upon a time I was attractive.

My sister is frightened. Her job demands a lot of her and she is trying hard to do it well. I should put her mind at ease, but I refuse because that will leave me all alone in this.

I eat too much and worry that I'm getting fat. I won't allow myself even one guiltless moment of pleasure around food.

When I come home I want to be alone.

I feel as if I have no friends.

No fun.

No life.

I'm tired.

I'm tired of being tired.

And tired of taking care.

Why don't they get it over with and die?

Joel saw me crying and he wrapped me in his arms and kissed my face and rubbed my back and smoothed my hair. He wanted me to love him. I was scared.

"We can't. You have a cold. Suppose I get it?"

We made love anyway.

Perhaps, because my mind was overtired, it quit. And then perhaps, because it quit, my body came alive.

Anyway, I was surprised.

I wasn't dead.

And it was nice.

I slept for six hours straight.

Some kind of record.

March 21 - April 1

The trip from hospital to home was tiring for Mother. She nodded in the car. As she went upstairs she had to stop on every step to catch her breath. She all but dragged herself to Billy's room and fell exhausted on the bed.

"I can't remember the name of the psychiatrist," she said with panic in her voice. "The one who said I wasn't crazy."

"Dr. Feldman?"

"That's it. Thanks."

She looked hollow-eyed and terrified: of how she felt, of what she could and couldn't keep in mind.

"I hate to bother you, but when you're free would you come upstairs and help me figure out my medicines? I have so many that I can't remember what I have to take."

I made a list.

She made apologies.

"I feel so bad," she said. "I so much didn't want to burden you."

I took her hands. "This is what I *want* to do," I said. "I want you here until you're strong enough to take care of yourself. Until the numbers stop. Then I'll kick you out, I swear. But in the meantime, I am glad that I can do it."

It was true.

"As long as you'll be making meals," my father said as I was making up a shopping list, "would you try to feed me foods that aren't fattening?"

Diet number ninety-nine.

"Of course. If you will promise not to cheat."

"Of course," he said.

Of course.

"What's *this?*" he said at his first lunch on my regime. He didn't look at me. He watched his busy fork exploring unfamiliar worlds.

"It's tuna fish," I said. "Without the mayonnaise Mother always drowns it in. I used just lemon juice instead, and lots of greens: iceberg lettuce, spinach, and watercress. They help to fill you up."

"They give me gas," he said. "Could I have some bread and butter, and a bit of mayonnaise? I only want to diet, not to die."

I tried to talk him into exercise.

"I'm going to run this afternoon, Daddy. Why don't you come to the track with me and walk around it a few times? Once you get your juices going you'll feel great! I guarantee it."

Ten steps up the slightly hilly street and he can't breathe. He huffs and puffs.

"Are you okay? You want to stop?"

"Not yet," he says. "It's just that I'm not used to climbing mountains."

"Then let's slow down," I say, although we can't. Slower would be stopped.

He strains. I talk about the good he's doing to his cardio-

116

vascular system, about the way he ought to walk with me each day as long as Mother's there so that "walking will be part of your routine and then, before you know it . . ."

He is not attentive.

"I'm going back," he gasps. "My chest hurts and my legs are killing me. You go ahead and run."

I do not trust that he will make it back alone. Together we hobble down the hill.

Most of the men I know with ailing parents rely on sisters, cousins, aunts, and wives to do the caretaking. They haven't got the time, they say, or the experience. Nor, I bet, do they receive support from friends who have done it, too, friends who know how hard it is.

"You poor thing," Debbie said to me the day I brought Mom home.

No tips on how to hold my upper lip or where to put my chin, just soothing sympathy.

"Poor thing. You must be beat. This has been so hard on you."

Ina showed up with a roast beef, cooked and sliced. "This is dinner for tomorrow night," she said. "On Saturday I'll make a load of chicken for the weekend."

Jackie called to say, "Count on me for Tuesday afternoon. Make plans to do something for yourself. I want to spend some time with your mother; so tell her, even if she doesn't feel like talking, I'll be glad to sit with her. And you'll get some time away."

Judy came by with a plant and its story:

"Last year, when Ivan's father was very sick and not expected to recover, I had a ready-to-bloom amaryllis plant at home that I took to his hospital room. As it blossomed, he got better. Now I have *this* one that's nearly in flower, and I want to give it to your mother."

My friend Lee, the movement therapist, had never met my mom. Nonetheless she said, "I'm coming by on Thursday after work. I'd like to see if I can get your mother to do some body work with me. It might help ease some stress if I can get her moving. I won't push her, but I think that I might help."

Friends.

It makes a female chauvinist of me to see the way women rally round. I wish that men could do it, too. Eventually, I think, because of two-job families and single-parent homes, they will. But in the meantime, let my two sons avoid the macho mold, I pray. As I decline, I do not want to contemplate confinement in a nursing home.

From the window at my kitchen sink I see my parents sitting on the chairs that Richie took outside. They are wrapped in winter coats, their sallow faces pointed toward the sun; their bodies hold the stiff and careful posture of the frail. They look exactly like a Medicare version of American Gothic.

Poor souls. They are so sick. How can they stand it? I wonder if they're scared to die and if they're sad—my once-upon-a-good-time-Charlie Dad and Mom.

How come *they* aren't crying?

That night I found one of my books on Mother's bed, *Facing Death* by Robert E. Kavanaugh.

"Is this the kind of stuff you read for class on Tuesday nights?" she asked.

I nodded.

"Is it any good?"

I shrugged.

"Tell me."

I talked to her about Elaine, whose story I had read for Death and Dying class the night before. Elaine described how she had come to terms with imminent death.

"Would you read it to me, please?"

Two months earlier I would have sold a limb for such an opportunity! Imagine: Mom and me and death and dying face-to-face!

118

Now it didn't seem so big a deal.

"Are you sure you want to hear it?"

"Yes."

She leaned against the pillows, closed her eyes, and listened to Elaine, a thirty-seven-year-old terminal cancer patient, talk about her lack of fear, her readiness for death, and the way impending doom had added depth to life. She avowed that she was, finally, aware of much more beauty in the world and infused with much more love and . . .

"I don't believe a word of it," Mom said. "It's bull."

"But it sounds like *she* believes it."

"That could be. But *she* is not my problem. Nor am I, right now. Or even you or Alice. I'm thinking about Daddy and how hard it will be for him after I'm gone. What will he do? Who will take care of him?"

A tear rolled down her cheek. "But I can't cry," she said. "Not now."

"Then can you sleep?"

"Probably. As long as sixes don't come up. Good night."

She sleeps. At least she doesn't stir. It's quiet. No one makes apologies.

If she says that she is sorry or she thanks me one more time . . .

I will not run tomorrow. My feet are sore. My body is stiff. I'm tired. Oh, the prison of my skin.

She can barely move. Daddy says his legs hurt when he takes five steps. And I complain.

Word of Arnold's sudden death the night before comes to us as we are eating breakfast.

"He was lucky," Mother says while buttering a cracker. "A very lucky man to die so fast."

"I guess," I say. And then, before my censor stops me, "But he didn't have the chance to do the growing and the getting close that you have done with us."

I hear the words too late. They are said. Where was my gag?

119

Mother laughs.

"You know," she says, "I think I might have lived quite happily without such an opportunity."

Not me.

Without the misery that led to Miriam, without the time to see my mother fighting hard to live, I might not have claimed a major part of her. I might not have known that she was someone I would like, in part, to be.

She runs the water for her bath. I hear the sound of breaking glass and dash upstairs to see my adolescent's medicated Stridex acne pads strewn across the bathroom floor and Mother—naked—in a crouch.

"Look how limber you are," I say, sounding like an idiotic Pollyanna. But I know what's coming and I do not want to hear it.

"I can't get the glass," she says. "I'm so sorry. All I am is trouble all the time."

My father calls. He is out of breath.

"What's wrong?" I ask.

"Nothing."

"Then why are you panting?"

"Because I've just been cleaning up and I'm so tired."

I lay out Mother's clothes. She dresses, lies down, and says, "I think I'll read."

She hasn't read for months.

"Read what?"

"That thing about Elaine's death wish."

She takes the book but is asleep before she can open it.

"See if Barbara wants my ticket for King Tut," I said to Judy. "There's no way I can take a day off in New York."

Judy would have none of my excuses.

"You stood in line two hours last September for those tickets," she chided me. "You really wanted to see the exhibition. With all the people who would gladly take a day to come and help out with your folks, if you don't go, you'd

120

better look damn hard at what you're doing to yourself. I think it looks a lot like wallowing," she said.

It wasn't that I saw the rightness of her argument. It was just that I didn't want to be thought a martyr. So I went and was amazed at what a train ride, a restaurant lunch, and the company of friends can do.

Something was brewing between my parents, something that made Mother talk more in numbers when my father came and when he didn't seemed to give her peace.

I brought it up at Miriam's.

"Four eights and seven greens," Mom said.

To which my dad replied, "I'm managing, but we will *have* to get some help when Mildred comes home."

"I'm scared more than he'll ever know," Mom said.

"There's nothing to be scared of," said my dad.

It was agreed that Mom would meet with Miriam alone the following week and then the week after she and Dad would go together. It was implied there were some things the children shouldn't know.

Oh, but I knew.

I knew the way she worried about him and how she couldn't stand the thought of him washing dishes or mopping floors.

How could she go home and watch him housekeep?

How could she go home and have a maid?

How could she go home?

Unless she settled it with him she never would.

Her thick, juicy cough came back. It worried me, but not the doctor.

"There isn't any evidence of cancer spread," he said. "As a matter of fact, your physical signs are stronger than they've been in a long time, Mildred. So you're getting the full dose of chemotherapy today."

"Oh, I'm so glad," said Mother in what, for her, was almost joy. She, who used to say she'd rather die than suffer chemotherapy, was giving thanks for the fullness of the dose.

Thus did she cling tenaciously to life.

Daddy called. She didn't want to talk to him. I told him she was sleeping.

"Please don't put me in between the two of you," I said as she was dressing.

She doubled over in a cough and started shaking hard. I had to grab two blankets, wrap her tightly in them, and hold her in my arms until she stopped.

We never settled it.

Next morning when I woke up, I started rocking myself back and forth.

How do I live out this thing? For so long I have thought that death was imminent. Suppose it's not?

I started shopping—for escape.

Mother was bathed, dressed, and stretched out on the sofa with the phone nearby and television on "for noise." I came into the den as if I had a thousand things to do and said, "I have to run some errands. I'll be back in time to fix you lunch. Do you mind?"

"Take it easy, breathless," Mother said. "And take your time."

I would go to Lord & Taylor or to Saks or anyplace with dressing rooms where I could hide out for a time, trying on clothes I wouldn't buy. With the life I was leading, denim more than met my fashion needs. I didn't need new clothes, and if I did, I wasn't apt to find them, for pale and tired as I was, everything looked bad on me.

But I wasn't out to buy. Just to be out. No wonder.

Her voice got babyish. Her chest was still congested and when she made the slightest move she wheezed or coughed.

She was all apologies again, and thanks.

There were numbers only now and then, but there were repetitions, questions, and forgettings.

"What was the name of the psychiatrist who said I wasn't crazy?"

"Remember how at Miriam's we said that when you get forgetful and talk in numbers or you whine we think it could be that you're scared?"

"Maybe I am," she said. "Maybe I am very, very scared."

Her tiny body trembled and I held her.

"I want to cry," she said. "I can't."

"Cry," I told her. "It will clear your head."

"I'll try," she said. "I'm trying so goddamned hard."

"Don't try so hard," I said.

Do. Don't. Cry. Try.

As if I knew what I was saying.

Since last September, with the start of chemotherapy and Daddy's stroke and me so often on the edge of panic, reflection had been a luxury I hadn't much indulged. There wasn't time. Thus, when I saw myself by turns as fool or bitch, or saint, I simply had to try to learn to stand it. There wasn't time to try for understanding. There always was too much to do.

But it's worth noting here that not one of the philosophic litanies I had memorized throughout my life was any help.

"Nothing human is alien to me," for instance, was unquestionably true. But knowing I could be a witch did not make me one whit more accepting of myself. Or change the way I acted.

Today I screamed at her.
Forgive me, God.

"Do you hear the way you're breathing, Mom?" I asked.

She shrugged.

123

"It sounds as if you're struggling for air. Is that what's happening?"

"Who knows?"

"Well, maybe it's a habit. Maybe you should pay attention."

"But look," she said with pride, "I'm dressed."

"But that's not . . ."

Her mouth was full of sores, she said. The cough was killing her. She didn't know how long she could go on.

Nor I.

"I'm going to call the doctor," Mother said.

"I don't want to bother Dr. Daniels, Barbara," I heard Mother say. "But I know he's going away and I think he ought to know I'm very weak and coughing and I'm tired."

Silence.

"Oh, thank you, Barbara. Thank you . . . thank you . . . thanks a million. Yes, of course."

She sounded like a grateful little girl, not like anybody's mother.

"He'll call me back," she said.

All afternoon she coughed and tried to hide it. "I hate to bother you," she said each time I brought a cup of tea or anything to soothe her throat.

"My God. You've got a cough. It isn't leprosy, and it's not your fault."

"I know, but I'm so sorry."

Barbara called at five-fifteen to say that Dr. Daniels wanted Mother put on tetracyclene and he wished to speak to her. I put her on the phone.

She waits. She greets the doctor, says a word or two, and listens. There is a long silence, and then, finally, she speaks.

"Oh, thank you, Dr. Daniels. Yes, of course, I will. And thank you, thank you. Have a good vacation and I'll see you in two weeks and thanks so much again for getting back to me."

I shriek. "Jesus Christ—stop groveling! It's not your fault

you're sick. You're not the guilty one. And what the hell are you thanking him for? He's your *doctor!*"

Mother cringes. Stares at me. Is mute. She blinks back tears. The awful silence lets me see myself.

"Oh, Mother." I have gone from hating her to wishing I were dead. "I'm so sorry that I yelled at you." I hold her. "But I can't stand to see you acting like a beggar. Being grateful for what is just your due. You're sick. You aren't bad."

"I know. But all my life . . ."

"I'm so sorry." I am crying. She is soothing me.

"This is hard for all of us," she says.

Hard.
I try my best. I really do. And still I screamed.
If nothing human is alien to me, it damned well ought to be.

Since Mother bathed, dressed, fed herself, and moved alone, albeit very slowly, I managed without household help. But I had to find someone to go with her when she went home.

There were four answers to my ad. Three respondents gave me longer lists of things they wouldn't do than would; the fourth had rotten references.

Suppose . . . suppose . . . there's only . . . always . . . me? . . .

I saw a Situation Wanted ad and answered it. The woman— Phyllis—liked the sound of me and I the sound of her. Now, I thought, I have to get Mom not to blow it with her crazy cleanliness demands.

"Don't worry," Mother said. "I'm more interested in kindness than cleanliness these days."

Did being put on medication make her think infection and not cancer caused the cough? Or was it me? Did she think I wouldn't yell so passionately at someone close to death?

Or—please don't let it be, I prayed—did she take my screams to mean I couldn't stand her anymore?

Any one or some or all of the above, I guess. But on Saturday, March 31, at Miriam's, my mother grabbed her life back.

It was beautiful to see. She was greedy—like a child. But she was like an adult, too.

"I want my own life. Now," she said. "I want to see my friends again. I want *my* home. *My* phone. *My* time."

The room was filled with energy. I loved it.

She turned to me. "You have been more wonderful to me than I can say, and I'm very grateful. But it's time. It's not because you yelled the other day. I know you love me. I love you. But it is time."

She turned to Daddy: "If Sy is willing I would like him to take me into town from here. We'll spend a little time in the apartment. Then I'd like to go to lunch with him. And then . . . we'll see. . . ."

She talked about the future. Things to do . . .

What had happened?

"I'm going home today," Mother said next morning.

"Today?"

"Today."

Yesterday convinced her she could count on Dad. The apartment, she said proudly, was amazing. "He really did a job."

Without, it seemed, a loss of manhood.

"You've been wonderful. You and Joel and the boys, but I'm going home."

126

April-September 1979

The past six months had so accustomed me to tending that I couldn't visualize a future where I wasn't running things or being utterly fatigued or near hysteria.

Only later would I see my mother's going home as the temporary start of relative peace.

"Do you miss me?" Mother teased.

"Yes," I said. "But I haven't had much time to think about it. I'm busy. And you? Do you miss me?"

"I do," she said. "But I am busy, too."

She left on Sunday, and on Monday, after both my folks swore up and down that they could make it through the day without me or my errands or my food, I turned away from them to other duties. I converted the house from nursing home to all-American cliché so that a high-school exchange student from West Berlin—due on Thursday night for a two-week stay—would know firsthand how wonderful the U.S.A.

and Jews really were. Passover was but ten short days away and Billy would be coming home. I made plans for the Seder, invited my husband's brother Ted to come to dinner with his children; asked my mother-in-law, Mom, Dad, and Alice. I ordered matzoh, fish, and chicken, planned to get Haggadahs, got Joel to agree to lead a service, and checked on what I needed for the ritual plate. All I could remember were the bitter herbs—the symbol of our suffering.

Mother started going out to lunch and for walks again. She did her housework and didn't talk in numbers anymore. She liked the woman we had hired. "She's very kind," said Mother.

"No more worry about Levine's?"

"No. It's good to have someone here to help."

My father's sister Bea was ailing in the early part of April. When I called to ask her husband, Ben, if I could borrow prayer books for the Seder Wednesday night, he said, "Bea is having tests today. She's really feeling rotten."

I started to respond with sympathy for Bea, but something in Ben's tone told me not to rush to answer him, just listen.

He was tentative at first, tiptoeing very gingerly around "a silly list of discontents."

I listened.

"I shouldn't even *think* of silly peeves when she is sick like this," he said. "It's dumb."

He said he didn't want to burden me. "You've got too much yourself with both your parents. But sometimes . . ."

"Sometimes it is horrible for *you*," I said.

That pulled a plug. He gushed.

"I have to watch each word I say to her. She's never been so supersensitive before. And yet . . . even though I *know* she's sick and I understand that she's worried and she certainly has reason to be scared . . . I . . ."

As his voice trailed off I sensed the shame he felt about his negative feelings toward someone he loved. He was emotionally in knots, a clone of me, a mess.

"I know," I said.

I knew. I recognized that he was going through the phase of hating that the person labeled "patient" gets attention while the one who gives the care gets exhaustion and depression as rewards.

"And how about *you?*" I said. "It's goddamned hard for *you*, and it's even harder just to *talk* about how hard it is. Next to Aunt Bea's problems all the things you feel seem trivial and petty. But it feels like you're doing all the work and plenty of the suffering and no one even *asks* how you are doing. No one seems to know . . . nobody seems to care. . . ."

He breathed a gust of relief into the telephone.

"Thank you very much," he said. "I feel much better now. Just to have you listen, just to talk about it helped a lot. I really feel much better."

It's a respite, Ben. A bit of peace, destined to be too brief unless Aunt Beatrice hurries up and heals. You don't get over Tending Syndrome, Ben, until the patient is well. Or unless the patient . . .

There's just remission, Uncle Ben.

There isn't any cure.

Mother was delighted not to need me, and pleased to be in charge of things herself.

"Now that Phyllis comes three days a week and I'm getting stronger, you don't have to worry anymore," she said. "I'm managing. Start living your own life, and try to write."

My visits became less frequent. Except for taking her to chemotherapy and making the "most welcome" frozen meal, I was officially reprieved. But, as for making target dates or putting time aside to write, it was impossible.

With my normal tendency to focus fitfully and be distracted easily—a result of years spent as a mother, combined with the past six months—I found that my attention span for things nonmedical was only slightly longer than a blink. I could not sit at a desk and do a thing that needed thought or

129

was sustained. The most I could manage, by then, was simply making order, sorting things but not sorting things out. Unable to make sense of things, I could at least make most things clean.

By then I was utterly my mother's daughter—relining drawers, organizing papers, scrubbing closet floors.

It was as if my mother followed me around my small two-story house and whispered, At last you've learned the lesson—only neatness counts.

Death and Dying class was coming to a close. Our final home assignment—designed to stress how short our time is and the importance of living according to our inner lights—was to write our eulogies and share them with the class on our last night together.

As the night ends, we are feeling close. Rose asks to speak to me, alone.

"When I first met you," she confides, "I thought your mother would be dead within a week. You looked and talked as if her end was a matter of days."

I nodded. "That's what I *thought*."

"Are you aware of how much you've changed in two short months?"

I shook my head.

"Well, I want to share with you what I perceive," she said. "You haven't mentioned anything about how hard it is for you in at least four weeks. You're laughing more. And two weeks ago you started wearing lipstick."

I must have been in mourning and not known.

Family therapy was moved from Saturday in Chestnut Hill to Wednesday afternoon in center city. Alice couldn't come midworking day, which pleased her very much.

"I'm overtherapied," she said. "And I'm sick of all the talk. I'll come if there's a problem, but if not, you won't be seeing much of me."

The sessions were reduced to two a month. I went to the first few, but what arose had more to do with Mom and Dad than Mom and Dad and me—and *most* to do with Mother.

Miriam agreed.

"It's perfectly all right if you don't come," she said to me. "But if you need me, I will be available for you or any member of the family."

Soon Mother was meeting alone with Miriam.

The space that Miriam encouraged me to make between my parents and myself was growing: I went less often to their place; I left them to themselves in therapy. But like the adolescent who believes she has to hate her family to make the necessary break, I spent much of the spring resenting them again.

"Daddy told me I should buy myself some clothes," my sister said.

He didn't say a thing to me, I wrote.

"I'm worried about Ethel," Mother said. "Life can be so lonely for a widow."

She never worries about me.

My notes were full of classic whines again:

If I don't phone them, they don't call me. (Am I turning into my Jewish mother's Jewish mother?) Why won't he ask me what I think? Why won't she stop the endless questions? Why can't I receive the unqualified approval she gives to Miriam? All I hear from her is "Miriam is beautiful" and "Miriam is kind."

I organized my recipes one day. Clipping and stapling I credited each to its creator—usually Aunt Emily or Bea.

Why didn't I have one recipe from my mother? Why didn't I have directions for a chocolate roll from Mom instead of facts about clean rags and instructions for the washing of wool sweaters?

Why hadn't she been more like other people's mothers?

And yet . . .

"What's wrong?" she says to me as we wait for the doctor.

The light blue paper gown is wrapped around her tiny frame. She sits on the table, leaning against the wall.

"Something is wrong," she says. "I see it in your face. I always know—with you—when something's wrong. Did something happen to the boys?"

I shake my head.

"God forbid a million times. What's wrong?"

She is weak and tired; the pins and needles in her arms and hands won't stop; there's back pain now and she is dizzy and increasingly unsteady on her feet. How dare I let her see that something as trivial as wallpaper is making me insane?

Besides, the last thing I want to hear is what I ought to do, or (Mother's panacea) whom I ought to sue.

"I'll tell you if you *promise* not to tell me what to do," I say.

She nods.

"You know we're papering the dining room," I say. "Well, the paper hanger found that we're two rolls short. So I called the paper company to order two more rolls and they told me that the smallest order they'll accept is ten rolls at a time."

"You mean . . ."

Just telling it could turn me purple.

"Ten goddamned rolls! To do two goddamned feet of wall!"

"Relax," my mother said.

"I called them twice, and Joel called them, too. But the company has 'rules' and they were not impressed with threats of lawyers."

She listened and she clucked commiseration. She must have had an inner fit not telling me to litigate, but all she did was say:

"Don't let it make you crazy, dear. God forbid a million

times . . . it could be something major. It's only money. Besides, it's not as bad as the Phillies' loss last night: eleven nothing."

Such was Mother's comfort.

I went into the hall, half laughing and half looking for the doctor, half wishing Mom knew what to *do* to solve my problem instead of every score of every goddamned game.

Sherry, the technician, hurried by.

"How's your mother feeling?" she inquired.

"Pretty much the same."

"You know," she said, "your mother is amazing."

I must have looked surprised.

"I see a lot of women with her disease, Diane. She really is remarkable. She won't complain. She takes pride in her appearance. You can see the pains she takes to dress and fix her face. What's more, she never fails to ask about me and my family and all the other people in this office. She manages to laugh—and mostly at herself. You should see the bitches who come in and do nothing but complain about their lives. She's really quite a lady. Quite amazing."

"That's nice to hear," I said. "I'll tell her what you said. And thanks."

"That's okay. But I wanted *you* to know it, too."

I do.

And yet . . .

She wants such Jewish-mother things for me. She tells me to "be careful" all the time. She tells me to "relax" and "take it easy."

"Easy's not my goal," I say one morning on my way to run. "I want to *do*, not lie around."

I do not say I do not want to be like *you*.

"You do enough. Besides, why do you have to run? You've got a car."

Annoying as she can be at times, she also makes me laugh.

And she continues to amaze me.

"How do you *do* it, Mom?" I asked her after Dr. Daniels ordered another X-ray of her cervical spine because she had such peculiar symptoms in her hands and fingertips.

"How do you manage to stay interested in other things? How do you stand the constant feeling rotten and the shrinking life? What's left that gives you pleasure anymore?"

"My family. You and Alice. Daddy and the boys. The fact that I can clean and do my work and make a home. And knowing I don't lie in bed and moan about my fate."

Not chocolate cake, exactly, but not bad.

"We" still went to chemotherapy twice a month. I still captained all the X-rays, scans, and tests. But after weeks of what I thought of as wasting time—and *now* see as decompression—I gradually began to live as if a parent's death was not an imminent event. I started living *my* life first again.

I did more mothering.

Bill planned six weeks abroad—three weeks in Europe and three in England studying medieval history. I helped him plan his trip. I shopped with him for what would wash and wear. Rich wanted summer work interspersed with wrestling camps and an Outward Bound trip as well. We talked about his choices, settled schedules, went together to buy hiking boots.

I happily went back to *normal* nagging.

I began cooking again—for pleasure. I saw my friends, took walks with some, had others in for dinner. I made plans without the caveats, and in mid-July, I started to put time aside to write.

During the mornings I was not on medical call, I started sitting at my desk for three hours at a time.

Mother's weak.
She's wobbly.

134

She's sleeping quite a lot.
Has pain.

I still recorded symptoms, both for my notes and for the doctor.

Her neck is sore.
She's dizzy and unsteady on her feet. She ate lunch with Mae and Claire today and they had to help her home because she couldn't navigate alone.
My father's walk is wrong. He says his legs feel strange.

But my mental state was less hysterical than it had been. I was more "sensible," less apt to panic at a parent's twinge. My mother's pains no longer led me straight to thoughts of catafalques; Daddy's headaches didn't always trigger my embalming fantasies. I had undergone a subtle, but major alteration in perspective: my focus switched from crisis into limbo.

I became a little more accustomed to my mother's suffering; a little more inured to my father's shortness of breath.

I became—in other words—more adept at standing their pain. In other words, I became a whole lot harder.

Today I tell myself that that was what I *had* to do in order to survive.

We wait in X-ray on a day in May, June, July, or August for pictures of a spine or neck or chest, for scans of brain or bone or liver.

Mom's eyes are closed again. She leans her scarf-wrapped head ("the wig's too godamned hot") against the paneled wall and sleeps while I protect her bag and try to make some notes.

It is the noise that gets to me today.

It is the retch, the slamming door, the cough that comes from around the corner. It is the click of keys, the clang of

135

gurney wheels along the tile floor, the ping of the arriving elevator. It is the oily voice of an operator paging Dr. Stevens on the intercom to "call three-eight-six-nine" and the cloying sweetness of another who wants "Extern Scap, at once, on eight-four-six."

It is the nurse who shouts into the waiting room, "Mr. B., you can go home now . . . Mr. B.," or who wants Mr. C. to "Come with me at once!"

It is the din that is a mirror of my inner state. I hate it.

Please, I pray, some peace.

Mother blinks and I look hungrily at anyone in white who passes by.

We wait.

A man as thin and black as licorice strings sits across from me and reads the New York *Daily News*. The paper falls from his shaking hands and as I move to pick it up, he screams at me:

"No! You go away. I used to do a hundred pushups every day at One hundred thirty-first and Lenox. I don't need *you* to do it for me. Besides, you got to die all by yourself, you know."

I back away.

I have not the slightest notion *how* you have to die.

Next to me a woman is rocking in her seat and humming "Rock of Ages." Down the hall a child cries. The intercom continues, a computer whirs, a typewriter carriage shifts . . .

"Shut up!" I want to scream. "Be still! We need some peace."

My mother sighs.

I rise.

"My mother's awfully tired," I tell the woman at the desk who seems to be in charge. "Is there any way? . . ."

"No," the ice maiden answers. "She will have to wait. Like everybody else."

But she's not like everybody else.

Ask Sherry.

"Do you think it will be long?" I say.

136

"I do not know."

She loathes me.

"Now, will you please sit down and wait? We'll get to you as soon as we are able."

Everybody waited then. It was the time of long and angry early-morning lines for gasoline.

Everybody hated the oil companies back then.

Not me.

I hated flabby, fair-skinned, blue-haired, wrinkle-fingered, tight-lipped Mrs. L. who said, through gritted teeth, "We'll get to you" as if it didn't matter that my mother suffered so.

I must take her name, I think. Report her.

Where?

To whom?

It isn't fair, I whine inside my head.

Fair?

What's fair?

Besides, it isn't *fair* I want.

It's *first*.

The wretched Mrs. L. was an exception to the people on my parents' medical team.

At Pennsylvania Hospital—their home away from home—sympathy and manners mixed with medicine were commonplace; it was a *given* that anyone on staff would be a kindly soul.

The same was true of Dr. Daniels and his busy crew. Not once were they abrupt or cold. As if to compensate for all the long, frustrating waits, they stayed consistently good-natured, unfailingly polite.

The women in Reception not only didn't come apart when twelve phones rang at once and lines formed at the desk to make appointments for times that were already triple booked, but when the doctor called them on the intercom while someone from the lab asked for a folder, they managed to stay pleasant through it all.

The lab technicians treated Mother like a queen. They propped her up with laughs each time they took her blood; they gave her love along with chemotherapy. They fed her questions about Bill and Rich, nourished her with compliments for Alice and for me. Sherry—when she saw that Mother had lost two pounds in one week—marched into the crowded waiting room and sat at Mother's feet to suggest that milkshakes taken late at night might add some weight. She named a dietary supplement.

"Ask Dr. Daniels what he thinks of Nutrament," she said.

"I hate to bother him with questions about food. He's busy," Mother said.

"He's your *doctor*," Sherry urged. "You can ask him anything you like. And remember, you are *not* a bother."

The bookkeeper, Resa, simplified the Medicare process. I signed my mother's name on the form and Resa filed it for me. She never failed to ask how *both* my folks were doing.

The doctor's medical assistants were always comforting. They listened sympathetically, never got a message wrong, and always called me back. If I so much as hinted at emergency, they put me through at once. Although their job was, partially, to shield the doctor, they made me feel connected to him, and protected.

Dr. Daniels, week after week, remained gentle, interested, and thorough, and, to my surprise, *accessible* behind his brisk facade.

"I don't know if she told you, but your mother called me after her last visit," he said one morning before starting the exam.

I nodded. I knew what she had done and I approved.

"She called to say she sometimes feels I am too quick for her. She said she knows she often isn't clear enough about her symptoms and she sometimes feels that I'm impatient and annoyed. But she said she wants me to remember that it's hard for her to list all the things that bother her. And sometimes she's ashamed and doesn't want me to think that she's complaining."

He had got it right.

"I'm very glad she told me," he said and turned to Mom. "I thank you once again, Mildred. Sometimes I *am* too quick. And if I seem impatient it's because I want to *know* precisely how you feel so I can help. But that's not the point. I am sorry that you feel that way, but very glad you told me. I will try to go slower."

He didn't like the way things looked on August 6.

"I'm dopey and I'm dizzy," Mother told him. "I'm dropping things, and the tingling in my arms is horrible."

Flat on her back she told him, "This is my only good position."

He took a long time testing strength and sensitivity in Mother's arms and legs. "Move your thumb as quickly as you can back and forth along the tips of the other fingers, Mildred dear," he said.

She strained.

He shook his head.

"That isn't very good at all. Is it hard for you to comb your hair?"

She ran her fingers through the salt and pepper strings her scalp had sprouted. "You call this *hair?*" she asked.

He shrugged. "I guess you have a point."

The latest brain scan was clear, he recollected. And the bone scan was substantially unchanged, except for one slight area around the sternum which was not significant.

"But the neuropathy concerns me. It *might* be arthritis," he declared. "But it *might* be spread of tumor to the spinal cord. I want her seen—this week—by Dr. Cook."

Ten floors below Cook's office, jackhammers shook and screamed. A radio was blaring while the workers repaired sewer lines.

Can as much be done for Mother as for Spruce Street sewage pipes?

Cook talked and tested, read charts and recapitulated.

First, there *was* arthritis in the neck, in addition to the tumor in two vertebrae. Some of Mom's responses had definitely changed; the X-ray, happily, had not.

Second, there was more spasm in the neck than he had observed last visit.

Third, reflexes in the arm were absent.

"I cannot say if any of these changes are caused by tumor spread. I don't know."

He prescribed a molded plastic collar to immobilize the neck which, along with Mother's wig, would surely keep her temperature fifteen degrees above the city's hot and humid normal. He put her on a higher dose of Elavil to "possibly decrease nerve firing."

"And," he warned, "if there is any increase in your weakness, I must see you right away."

"I will cooperate with you one hundred percent," Mom said. "How else can I expect to beat this thing?"

I had planned—if Mom and Dad were well enough—to take them out to lunch post Dr. Cook. They needed more distractions, so I thought I'd introduce a pleasant change into their day.

"I read about a restaurant near the hospital," I said. "It's called the Celery Stalk. Do you think you'd like to try it?"

They agreed.

Inching toward the restaurant, I tried to recall exactly what the review had said about the place. All I could remember was that it sounded good to me.

On entering, I knew why: the specialties were salads, whole-grain breads, fresh fruits, thick—meatless—soups, and yogurt drinks. All things *I* love to eat, but the makings of a famine for my folks. Nowhere was the Russian dressing or the coleslaw for the corned beef that they loved to have midday.

"Let's go," I said. "It's a mistake."

"No. We'll be okay. Let's just get a table," Mother said. "I really need to sit."

Wrong place.

The Celery Stalk—a cafeteria—had clearly posted signs announcing stringent rules against reserving table space before you filled your tray.

"Look sick," I said to them. They looked at me and laughed. "Look sicker. That way you can sit and I'll go through the line and choose your lunches."

They looked at one another in a silence that was eloquent, conveying they would rather struggle through the line themselves than risk *my* choosing food.

"Go ahead," I said. "I'll sit and save a table. If anyone says anything, I'll show them whom I'm with."

Mom and Dad limped through the line. I watched them search among the spinach and the raw, unsalted nuts for something edible. They settled on a cold fruit soup, carrots drowned in crunchy dressing made with dill, and bread made out of vegetables.

The tray was hard for Mom to manage with her aching neck, her heavy bag, the ever-present cane. Dad's lousy balance made it difficult for him. I ran to the line's end, took each one's tray, and raced it to the table, where I thought I'd sit with them and skip *my* meal. The line was growing longer. The dose of fun would be too much.

"The line's too long," I said. "And I'm not really hungry. Instead of eating, I'll get the car while you're finishing."

"Relax," said Mother. "Don't be such a breeze. Relax and eat."

To my surprise, I did.

I see her shrivel, see my father slow. I hate the way their lives grow small.

But—still—I drop them off at their apartment and don't go in. They do not need me now.

Though I worry constantly about them, I still live.
I have my life.

Joel and I were planning a combination belated birthday-back-to-college-party on August 25 for Bill.

"Maybe we should have the party in a restaurant," I told Joel when I heard that friends from Boston would be coming in to stay with us that weekend. "I'd like to spend time with Herb and Roberta. Or maybe we should order trays of cold cuts. I'm not sure I want to cook for thirty kids—I'd rather use the time to write. Besides, Mother goes to chemotherapy, which means that Monday of that week is shot. And Richie's due back home the following week. I want to get his room in shape."

"Relax," my husband said. "I'll help."

"We" had chemotherapy on Monday. Mother's neck was sore and Daniels ordered X-rays. Tuesday I went marketing and made and froze a chicken dish and meatballs for the party. My parents came to dinner Tuesday night. Wednesday I bought paper goods and plastic knives and forks and began to bake the cookies and the cakes. It was Thursday when the stove blew up. Baking soda stopped the fire, but I had to throw away two half-baked cakes and find someone to fix the oven sooner than the following week because of all the baking that remained to be done. I was trying to wipe char off the wall behind the stove when Joel called to say that Rich had just phoned from Colorado to announce that he was leaving Outward Bound a week before the course was over because of blood clots and infection in his toes. Our friends arrived at nine that night. When they heard that Rich was coming home they said they would go to a motel.

"No. The boys can stay together. They won't care. And I don't mind at all," I lied.

Rich called at ten to say his plane would be arriving at nine-thirty the next night and that the nails on both his big toes were off.

142

Friday, August 24, was Mother's sixty-seventh birthday. I dared not take her present to her because I had to wait for the repairman who finally arrived at four o'clock. He saved the stove. I baked.

Richie looked okay, but he was hurting.

On Saturday at 8:00 A.M. I marketed for salad greens and extra cake, since five of Billy's friends—visitors sometime in the middle of the night—had eaten more than half of what I had made for Billy's party. I made a welcome-home breakfast of French toast for Rich, whose eyes were red from pain and lack of sleep.

My father called to tell me that my mother's legs were swollen.

Joel, dawdling over morning coffee, said, "How do you feel about my playing golf today?"

I wasn't shy.

I told him.

He didn't play golf.

Instead he fixed a window in the car, which took an hour and a half. He insisted that I show him where to go for beer and soda. He watched a soccer game on television, cleaned a bathroom, made our bed.

"Would you make some popcorn, please?" I said while he was recovering from the strain of straightening our comforter.

"Where do you keep it?" asked the passing stranger.

"Up—"

I despised him.

"Never mind."

Relax.

"I'll help."

DROP DEAD!

Mother took the news that Richie had come home and was in pain in character: she panicked.

"God forbid a million times," she screamed. "Is he all right?"

143

I had to reassure, to mother *her*, which I resented.
Richie needed care.
So did I.
She said to get our lawyer right away. "If anybody ever had an airtight case . . ."
Richie moans in agony. Codeine doesn't help the pain.
Joel and I were up three nights trying to give comfort and trying to contain our rage. All we did was visualize what must have happened on a Colorado mountaintop to give our child frostbite.

Richie's feet are up.
Mother's ankles, fat.
He hurts.
She's miserable.
Billy wanders in and out. I ask him motherly questions, which he detests.
He's eager to get back to school.
He wants to be away from here.
Me, too.
The air is thick with silence between Joel and me. Fury brings us close at night when Richie moans in pain, but my resentment over his "helping" me last weekend runs through every day.
I cannot stand my child's pain.

Rich was hospitalized on Labor Day to help control the pain. An electromyogram showed damage to the nerves in his feet.

"We don't know much about frostbite in this part of the country," the doctor said. "But I can assure you that your son won't lose his toes. And I promise that his pain *will* ease. It may take some time, however. I also think he should stay here until we break the pain cycle."

Next day Dr. Daniels called to say he wanted Mother to see Dr. Cook again and Joel's mother said her field of vision now included a mysterious black dot that wouldn't go away. My brother-in-law Ted stopped by to announce that he was getting sick and Daddy said his chest pains were much better recently, but there was something in his belly . . .

I closed the windows, turned on the air conditioners to cover all the noise I knew I'd make, and cried.

"I cannot stand my child's pain. I'm tired of disease. I'm sick to death of sickness and of things I cannot fix."

I pleaded for MY life six months ago.
 I've got it now.
 It stinks.

October 1979 – August 1980

The doctor wanted Mother in the hospital again.

"I want Dr. Cook and Dr. Simeone—a neurosurgeon—to examine her," he said.

She had a growing weakness in her legs, a positive Babinski reflex in one foot, and frequent dizzy spells.

"They'll want to do a myelogram to see if something's pressing on her spine," he said. "They'll do another EEG. We'll take an X-ray of her spine again, and I want to run some other tests."

October first.

"You're forty-three today," she said, obediently lying flat.

"I'm forty-four."

Good Christ! She doesn't even know my age!

"I'd swear that you are forty-three. I guess I lost a year."

Maybe just sight of me.

"What are you doing to celebrate?" she said.

"Having dinner with Aunt Emily and Daddy."

I always feel inadequate when people tell me that they've "gotten things resolved" or "worked through" all their "issues." No matter how *I* try I never get beyond uptight in certain secret places of my mind. The only inner alterations I've achieved are very little shifts, and only intermittent ones at that. The only change, in fact, I've ever seen as permanent and major in myself is that I—sometimes—can accept *some* contradictions.

Thus could I write and not be too consumed with guilt:

She's in the hospital again . . . the poor, sad, wretched soul.

And three lines down complain:

Son of a bitch! She will not even let me have my birthday free of worry.

The doctor's verdict—"no significant change"—was good, but puzzling. Something "not significant" seems trivial. But can a cancer spread—however small—be seen as unimportant?

What didn't bother Mother's doctor bothered me—and must have bothered Mother even more.

Joel's annual convention—in Phoenix, on November 4—gave us an opportunity to spend three days in Bryce and Zion national parks. That area of Utah is a favorite place for me. I love the red-brown rocks, their eerie shapes, the stained-glass sky, the quiet.

I couldn't wait.

Day one away I caught a cold. My ears were stuffed, my throat was sore, I ached. While Joel took a ranger-guided hiking tour through Zion, I lay in bed and shook. I barely managed a brief stagger around the rims of Bryce, day two; mostly I complained. The pain—a fire in my sternum—started at midnight in Sedona, Arizona. It was a burning,

147

clenching, radiating hurt that wouldn't stop. I tried to meditate the agony away, but when that failed, I crawled into the bathroom, lay on the cooling tile floor, and moaned until I managed to wake Joel.

He sympathized; he patted me. He talked and tried to soothe, but nothing helped. Within three writhing hours we were heading for a hospital in Phoenix.

St. Luke's.

Emergency.

The pain subsided as I entered, but I was weak, still sore, and very scared.

A nurse helped me undress. She put me on a table, took my vital signs, and stood by while an intern ruled out heart attack.

"The resident will be here soon," she crooned. "Try to relax."

We waited.

I thought about my blooming health for which I had never failed to thank the fates and realized that not only was it splendid to be always in the pink, but that it was—for me—a vital mark of separateness: Well, I was not like my parents. Especially not Mother.

Joel held my hand and when the pain returned he rubbed my belly and my forehead. He tried to comfort me the way I often tried to comfort Mother as she waited for *her* medical redeemer.

My God, I thought, my husband is being *me*. And I am Mom.

This time *I* am the patient on the table, vulnerable and weak. This time *I* am terrified that people won't be nice. ("Thank you, thank you, thank you," I had told the nurse and intern half a dozen times.) This time *I* am desperate to be liked.

The world began and ended with my flesh. I was sole guest inside a universe of hurt.

My God, I thought, I'm Mom.

Immediately, I realized my mistake.

My mother's every day brought some new pain, but *she* stayed interested in things that were not her: in politics, in sports. She had constant body problems, but she always got enough outside herself to *care* about her family and friends, to ask the loving question, and to laugh.

Not me.

I hurt and did not give a damn for anything but myself.

Oh, no, I am not my mother, I saw, not by a mile.

I am not made of such good stuff as she.

My "possible case of gallstones" disappeared and we proceeded, postconvention, south to Tucson where we spent three days with people who, like my mother-in-law, made growing old look good.

Our host was a handsome, active, vigorous man of eighty-four. His seventy-year-old wife, a gracious, open woman, had a flashing, teasing wit. They were interested in many things: in one another, us, Indians, politics, traveling, books.

The air around them was alive and stimulating.

I should have frozen it and flown it home.

Mother, with a bad cold and bronchitis, greeted me from bed when I returned. She had nearly been admitted to the hospital again, so close did pneumonia seem. My father had tripped on Market Street. His elbow, fortunately, broke the fall, but a sac of pus the size of a golf ball had formed on the joint, and if it didn't drain within a week or two, it would have to be removed surgically. A kid whom Richie wrestled stuck a finger in Richie's eye, and though there was *supposed* to be no damage, Rich complained that his vision sometimes blurred. Our friend Mortie's mother died. Aunt Emily, pushed, on purpose, by some hoods, fell and hurt her shoulder and her hip and she, who loved so much to walk, was sentenced to "at least three weeks in bed." Uncle Ben had polyps taken out; they were benign. But back at home, while mending, he developed fever and sharp pain, which sent him to the hospital again. Jessie, one of Judy's dearest friends, died. And Herman, walking briskly, looking optimistically ahead, felt something in his cuff, which was a cane. The blind man tumbled too.

Mother didn't ask me for another last Thanksgiving dinner, which was fine. I didn't want to play Perle Mesta this year. I wanted to be someone's guest.

My sister took me off the hook. "I'll have it here," she said.

The food was very good. My sister was a calm and gracious hostess.

It was a peculiar evening, though. Nobody had a fight.

"What is it about?" people started asking when they heard that I was working on a book.

"About caring for my ailing parents," I replied. "About how hard it is . . . how full of many feelings . . . about . . ."

I never got to "midlife crisis" or "family therapy" or anything else.

First came the knowing look, then the confessions:

"I've been taking care of Mother for four years. If I don't get away . . ."

"My father's in a nursing home. I can no longer stand to go to see him."

"My brother pays the bills and thinks, because he sends a monthly check, he's off the hook."

"If she only weren't so impossibly demanding . . ."

"I know," I'd say. "I sometimes feel . . ."

I rarely got to finish. Most people were so full of pain they couldn't wait to listen; they needed to unload.

"My father-in-law is emptying my life."

"My sister does it all and I feel guilty, but there's nothing I can do. I have a business. . . ."

"My wife does nothing but complain these days. . . ."

Most of us were so alike it was amazing. Except for the peculiar one or two:

". . . about how hard it is," I would declare. "How tiring. How full of rage and love and . . ."

"Rage?"

Lips would quiver into stiff and puzzled smiles, the backbone would tighten noticeably.

"What rage?" The head would shake. "I cared for Mother for three years—she lived with me and she was senile near the end. Not for one moment did I mind the things I had to do for her. It was a pleasure . . . constantly, I was never angry or resentful for a second."

Fortunately, I encountered few such out-of-touch responses.

Mostly we were all the same, intimately connected by our pain.

Memory revises.

I *recall* the time from November 1979 until September 1980—with no long and awful hospital stays, no near catastrophes—as a period of calm, a kind of a vacation.

But my *notes* remind me that aside from being much less tired and leading an outwardly more "normal" life, I was often sad and angry.

My diary for one day in December:

Picked Mother up at two this afternoon for three o'clock appointment with oncologist who Daniels wants to "reevaluate" her case.

Mom tells me in the car about a luncheon she'd like to attend tomorrow but won't because she isn't strong enough to stay the afternoon.

"Go," I say. "I'll drive you there and pick you up and bring you home as soon as lunch is done."

"But I don't want to inconvenience you," she says.

"Go," I tell her. "I don't mind. You don't have much fun these days. As long as you would like to go, I'd really like to see you do it. I'll be glad to pick you up. I mean it, Mother."

It was true.

"Thanks a million. I'm really grateful. I would like to see the girls. I hate to inconvenience you, but thanks a million."

I drop her off at the hospital. "Sit down and wait," I say. "I'll park and come right back and help you up."

I park and hurry back to Mom. We wait. The elevator takes forever. Finally, we get to five, where we have to wait some more.

When the nurse calls Mother's name, at last, we go to an examining room, she gets undressed, and then we wait again. The doctor arrives. He pokes, prods, and asks a hundred questions I appear to have the answers to.

Dates I know, and labels. But nothing that explains anything.

"I need more information," says the doctor. "I need to see old records and X-rays. Can you arrange to get them to me?"

I say I will have someone pick them up from Dr. Daniels in the morning and deliver them to Thirty-fourth and Spruce by 10:00 A.M. "Is that okay?"

"That's fine," he says. "You're very good. Dr. Daniels said you were amazing."

"She's wonderful," says Mom.

I help her dress and walk her down the hall. We have another elevator wait. I get the car, help her in, drop her off at home.

"Thanks a million," Mother says again. "You have been wonderful. You are an angel. Thanks."

Sometimes I think I'm not so bad.

Ah, but tonight:

When Joel asks about my day I start to cry and say, "It was horrible. I'm tired of all the waiting and Mother's pain. I'm sick of Mother's constant groveling to doctors. I want a normal life, but there's a beeper in my head that makes me feel I'm on constant medical call. All I'm really good for anymore is to drive and talk to doctors and to sit in waiting rooms all day."

I wrap my arms around my knees and start to rock.

I'm whimpering.

"This takes so goddamned long. It is a goddamned nightmare. I go two times a goddamned month for chemotherapy and why? I don't have cancer! Mother does! And she has had it long enough. I'm sick of it."

Sometimes I'd like to rip my skin away.

How do you "resolve" such things? How do you "work" such feelings through?

I never learned.

All I could do was proceed.

Mother's always sensitive antennae became more acute the longer she was ill. Sometimes she perceived resentments I had not yet felt.

"What's wrong?" she asked as I was fighting Monday morning traffic on our way to chemotherapy.

"We're going to be late," I said. "I'm nervous."

"That's not what I mean. You seemed annoyed at taking me. You know how much I hate to bother you like this. You know you do not *have* to do the driving. I can take a bus. I'd *rather* take a bus than have you mad at me. I'd rather *die* than burden you. . . ."

Oh, not the burden trip again, I thought.

And then: goddamnit, why not get it said?

"You're right," I said. "I am annoyed. I'm tired and I often wish I didn't have to do this all the time."

She winced.

"But that's just part of it."

I took her hand.

"The other part is knowing that even though it's hard for me, it's got to be a hundred times more difficult for you and I would rather do it than not. And yes, it sometimes *is* a burden, but so what?"

I told the truth.

We turned another corner.

But honesty was not enough.

Miriam called one Wednesday afternoon.

"Are things okay?" she asked.

"They're fair," I said. I told her how much my mother's misery could still annoy me. Even though I knew she couldn't help constantly feeling bad, it was so damnably depressing. Although so much between us was better, I still despised her lack of clarity, the way she thanked everyone too much, and wouldn't get a single story straight, and . . .

"Doesn't *anything* get permanently settled?" I asked Miriam.

She didn't answer.

"I am calling you because your mother says she thinks you're often angry, and she's uncomfortable."

A flash of fury grabbed me for a moment.

What does Mother want from me? I thought. How much must I give until she's satisfied? And how dare Miriam, who spent so many sessions telling me I should back off, call to suck me in again?

"How do you handle your anger?" Miriam asked.

How does one answer such a question without drowning in encounter talk, I wondered.

"Like everybody else," I said. "Sometimes well and sometimes not at all. Obviously, not well enough if you're calling me."

And what did "handle" mean? If it had to do with "working through" I was in trouble.

"I run. I try to use up angry energy on the track. Sometimes I write some rage away. I talk about it, now and then. But it never disappears and now and then I *still* explode. Clearly, if you're calling me, it's getting through to Mom."

"Not only that. Your mother doesn't think you and your father and your sister know how hard she's trying."

"I do," I said. "I think she's amazing. But there's a *me* in all of this that's torn, a me who wants a mother. *I* can't take away her pain . . . and . . ."

What was I supposed to do?

I stewed.

At Miriam.

At Mother.

How much? . . . How dare? . . . What did everybody want from me?

And then, inevitably, I saw myself inside my mother's tired skin. That always did it. Poor Mom, I thought. And cried.

And then I called.

"Miriam said you feel as if I do not know how hard you're trying, Mom. I do. But sometimes all I have is how it is for *me*. I'm sorry, but it's true. Please know that I am aware of how hard you're trying. I admire you so much. I love you."

We both felt better for a while, but nothing was "worked through."

Lunch with M., a friend whose mother-in-law has come to stay until a "place" for her—a nursing home? a rehabilitation center?—can be found.

"I hate her living in my house," says M. "I used to like her. Now I hate her, myself, and my husband, who marches off to work each morning and leaves me with the job of doing everything."

A nod from me.

"My whole life is flat," she says. "No fun. And my sex life is nonexistent. When I've finally gotten Mother into bed, I put on an old bathrobe, watch the dumbest thing that I can find on television, and don't even bother washing. I just collapse in bed. Occasionally, my husband pats me on the back. . . ."

"I know," I say.

"I'm making three meals a day again, as if my kids were little. And, speaking of my kids, I wanted to enjoy this last year with my daughter before she leaves for college. But how can I, when I'm exhausted all the time and irritable? . . ."

We only change the names.

"I know what you are going through," I say.

And though the knowing cannot possibly make life less difficult for M., it seems to comfort her.

We speak with little shame. We talk about the worry and jealousy we feel, the anger and fatigue, the love and pettiness. We talk about how long things take and then we go beyond complaints to talk of gratitude and duty, to take note of the good that we are doing. We mark the undercurrent running through these trying times: the knowledge that one day *we* may be the topic of a teary talk at lunch; the possibility that *we'll* someday be a burden to our children.

"But there are reasons to be pleased," I say, surprised at what I find I really think.

"You're doing good, you're being kind. No matter how you feel, you're *acting* well. That's worth a lot. Besides . . . it's not a bad example to be setting for your kids. . . ."

I sound as if I'm wise.

But what the hell, it's true.

Not all my interchanges were so sane.

At a wedding in December, I listened to a fifty-one-year-old woman talk about how wonderful her life was.

". . . and my kids are on their own and doing fine," she said. "And my husband and I finally have time . . ."

I nodded.

"I haven't felt this good . . ."

"Are both your parents living?" I burst in.

"No." She looked at me quizzically. "Mother died ten years ago and Dad, who ailed for years, just passed away last January."

"Who took care of him?" I said.

"My brother and I shared it."

"But mostly *you*, I bet?"

She nodded yes.

"Do you think your present happiness has anything to do

with the fact that you are free? That both your parents are dead?"

"My God!" she said. "I never thought of *that*."

She reeled away from me.

In a crowded supermarket late one Thursday afternoon, I stood in line behind a feeble white-haired woman who leaned weakly on her cart while a middle-aged man—her son—threw cans of fish and loaves of bread and bags of fruits and vegetables on the checkout counter. A younger woman held a bag of apples up and said, "Are you sure these are the kind of apples that you want, Mom?"

The old lady shrugged. "Whatever you think. What difference does it make?"

It made a difference to the daughter-in-law. Her body arched; her voice got hard and sharp. "You *have* to tell me what you want if I'm to help you," she insisted.

"But I don't care."

There it was again. Another family in the stew. An old lady weak and needy, but surely alert enough to sense the hatred in the body of the bitch her son had wed. Alert enough, too, no doubt to recognize her son's annoyance—loud in how he tossed the cans of food.

How she must have hated her dependence!

And the man and woman: weary. It was five-thirty. They might have both just finished work. All they wanted was to do their duty, get it over with quickly, and go back home and flop. Their kids were finally gone. For years they had looked forward to some time that might be theirs.

They probably were scared, too. Suppose her indifference marked the start of a new phase? More and more the aging woman wasn't caring about things. Suppose this meant she couldn't live alone much longer? What if she had to live with them?

Another family in the stew.

157

Only the names varied; at center we were all the self-ish same.

A hospice service—staffed by social workers, nurses, and physicians who wanted to relieve the shocks that failing flesh receives—was established at Pennsylvania Hospital in February 1979. Its purpose was to provide a range of services for the gravely ill—and for their families—for which a corps of volunteers needed to be recruited. These people would visit, listen, run the hundredth errand, read a book, or simply bring that comforting cup of tea.

With an expectation of doing volunteer work with the sick and old when Mom and Dad no longer "needed me" (I refused to think beyond the euphemism) I signed up for the Hospice Volunteer Training Program that was given on two Saturdays in January 1980.

Talk and films and talk about the history of the hospice movement. Talk about denial and Elisabeth Kübler-Ross. Talk of methadone and other kinds of pain control. Talk of spiritual needs and autopsies and symptoms.

Talk—in groups of course—about our feelings.

So long to sit. So many words, so unconnected to the things I've seen on wheels in the nuclear medicine department.

There is another thread, however: the warmth and kindness of the people who are leaders.

The lack of cant: there is less jargon here than I had feared.

The caring.

But all the talk.

How can so many words help someone who is hurting?

They can't.

The training is a way to screen the crazies.

I attended the two sessions, listened, took good notes, and wrote and mailed in my reactions as requested. I didn't make a date to have the private interview required prior to assignment, though.

I didn't plan to volunteer until later. . . .

Knee surgery for Rich, March 10.

A heavy cast.

Excruciating pain.

I cannot tell my mother how he hurts because she gets upset and then I have to comfort *her*. I can't complain about my days as constant chauffeur while Rich heals because she'll think my taking her to chemotherapy is an added chore—which it is—but who, if not myself, can do it now?

Alice, they remind me, "works."

I play.

We're seeing Dr. Keech this afternoon: a sweet, relaxed young fellow in Oncology and Hematology filling in for Dr. Daniels, who is away.

Mother lists her symptoms.

How brave she is, I think. However, I cannot stand to hear her rundown anymore: sore eyes, headaches, tired back and neck and knees, tingling sensations, dizziness, sores in her mouth. . . .

"I think you're doing very well," says Dr. Keech.

My father calls me early one morning two weeks later.

"I don't care what the doctor says," he says, "she's a mess."

She's weak, he tells me. And, although she tries her best, everything takes her increasingly longer and she won't let him help. She still goes out, but not so much for luncheon with her friends as for half an hour's change of scene and only once or twice a week. She's usually too tired.

"I don't care what the doctor says. She's losing ground."

"Call the doctor, Daddy," I suggest. "Tell him what *you* see."

My father calls me back at five o'clock.

"Dr. Daniels says he doesn't understand why mother is so weak. The recent X-rays only show the *slightest* spread," he said. "There isn't any change that is significant."

The tumor is a stowaway. Unless it travels to a capital upon the continent of Mom—the liver or the lungs—the doctors will not fuss. Little forays back and forth across a border—a cheekbone or a vertebra—they see as being of little consequence.

The doctors do not understand.

But Daddy knows.

And so do I.

She's dying.

Mother said she'd like to see Atlantic City.

"When?" I said. "Let's make a date."

"When I'm feeling better."

"Let's not wait until then. Let's do it Thursday."

"All right . . . if all is well. . . ."

"All won't be well. We'll do it anyway."

June 26. I pick them up at ten-fifteen. Daddy is dressed à la Las Vegas: light green slacks, a yellow shirt, a green and yellow jacket. Mother is in a two-piece copper-colored cotton Calvin Klein. Her hair is thin, but long enough to tie in two straggly bunches, which, despite my protestations, she will not undo.

She carries the inevitable bag of newspapers, but she walks more strongly to the car that's going to casinos than to the car that goes, on other days, to chemotherapy.

Something to look forward to . . .

I pick up my cousin Debbie. She comes because my parents like to be with her, and she with them. Also because she is my friend and her lively talk will occupy my folks and keep the strain of entertaining them from me.

I drive.

Debbie, as expected, talks. My mother listens. Daddy doesn't hear.

"For Christ's sake, Sy. Why don't you get a hearing aid?" yells Deb.

"What?" my father says.

We drop the car at Park Place valet parking, take an escalator up one flight, turn right, and enter a jazzed-up fairyland, bright with lights and mirrors in motion all the time, abuzz with the metallic noise of slot machines.

We arrange to meet an hour later.

My father and my cousin disappear.

I walk with Mother to a slot machine, she drops a quarter in, and loses, looks around and says, "I have to sit. This is too much for me."

But sitting is not what Park Place is about. The padded, backless benches don't invite long stays. "Play," they seem to say, "or leave."

"You can't sit *here* in comfort," I tell Mom.

"I'll be okay," says Mother. "You go and have some fun. I'm really fine."

I drop a quarter in a slot, win ten dollars, and quit. I check on Mom who says she's having fun just watching people come and go.

I can't find my father.

Debbie's playing seven slots at once. I help her rake the money in, check Mom who says she's still fine, and wait for one o'clock when Daddy reappears.

He is the Sy of old again—a winner. He is expansive, grand, a sport. He buys a banquet lunch for us.

It's fun.

And Debbie, bless her, keeps the conversation going.

She mentions someone's awful self-absorption.

"Let me tell you something," Daddy says. "At his age it's not unusual to be self-centered. All you really care about at seventy-three is yourself."

I take advantage of his honesty to stake a claim:

"That's true. Neither of you is interested in *me* too much," I say. "Not the way you used to be."

If Daddy hears he doesn't care. Mother nods in agreement.

My father recalls the death of a dear aunt when he was just sixteen:

"I was devastated," he says. "But other deaths became more frequent and, eventually, less terrible. You finally—at my age—almost take them in your stride. Except, I guess, for the death of a spouse. And even *that* grief's selfish."

Mother nods.

We walk slowly to the boardwalk. Mother waits on another bench while we three push ahead to peek in at Caesar's, which is mobbed. My father's face is turning red. "I've had it," he declares before he drops a cent. "We'd better go."

We collect Mom and then the car, which Debbie kindly drives because I'm tired, as are Mom and Dad.

But they had fun, and so did I.

Mother lost the vision in her right eye for fifteen minutes one night in July.

"Amaurosis fugax" was the diagnosis. "Fleeting blindness."

"Due to cancer?" I asked Dr. Cook.

"No. Due to a tiny blood clot that must have traveled from the carotid to the ophthalmic artery. In other words," he said, "your mother had a little stroke."

Don't be absurd. My *father* has the strokes. My mother has the *cancer*.

"The prognosis?" I inquired automatically. As if he knew. As if his words would make it true.

"That's hard to say," he said. "Your mother has so many things wrong with her that she could have another major stroke at any time, or nothing like this again for the rest of her life. There isn't any way to know. Let's just say it's a warning."

The ophthalmologist whom we consulted concurred.

"This episode—this tiny stroke—is not significant in and of itself," he said.

Nothing was significant, but all these things that did not mean much "in and of themselves" were killing her.

"But it has to be regarded as a warning. . . ."

As if we needed warnings. My mother had become a moving DEW line.

I'd kill myself.
I swear to God if I were half as sick as she, I'd kill myself.
What kind of life is it with constant worry, with something always wrong?
If I were she I'd kill myself.
I know it.

I wrote those words like a robot, repeating, automatically as blinking, exactly what I used to hear my parents say: "Let me get it over with. What's the big deal if I die?"

Their attitude toward death was cavalier, offhand. "I'd rather die than live like that" was Mother's verdict on life in a wheelchair, or with a missing limb. Life without sight was "not a life at all" she used to say. "You can be goddamned sure that I will kill myself if I'm not right. If *ever* I become a burden—to myself, or anyone—you can be sure I'll swallow pills. God forbid a million times, life's not that important. I'd rather die than be in any way impaired."

Life-denying words slid as glibly from my father's lips:

"What's the point of living if you are not at full capacity?" he'd say. "Don't ever hesitate to let me die if *any* of my faculties are gone."

They were so sure, so unafraid, so clear of eye and cool of head when what they said did not connect to them. But now I know it was a sham. Unconscious, but a con. As long as death was distant, they could disdain it. But see them when death threatened.

Mother does her work. She won't miss chemotherapy. She

struggles with a cane to climb aboard a bus in summer heat to get to Miriam to talk about the ways she might improve relations with her family.

"I've got to fight. I'm going to beat this goddamned thing."

When a stroke impaired my father's speech and sight he said, "I can't read *yet*, but you can bet your life I will. And my speech is getting clearer, don't you think?"

After his ataxia he gladly used a walker.

He is on a different diet every month. He tries to smoke low tar and nicotine cigarettes.

So much for what we say we will not take.

Kill myself?

Never.

Lest she should forget her tribulations for a second—forget the stroke, the tingling, the dizziness and pain—the gods took two of Mother's bottom teeth away, which meant, besides despising how she looked, she had to spend much of the summer with her mouth agape and her neck at an outrageous angle while a dentist mucked around a mouth so sore from chemotherapy a bridge could not be made to fit.

My dentist, who, in my experience, could do anything, was away until after Labor Day.

"Will you wait for Leonard Abrams?" I asked Mother. "I know he'll fit a bridge for you, and quickly, too."

"I'll wait. My missing teeth are not exactly interfering with my modeling career, but I sure would like to look less like a witch."

Another groin lump needed to be watched.

Dr. Daniels ordered a bone scan and asked the radiologist to "read past X-rays and compare for metastasized breast cancer."

Everything was going.

All was loss.

The cancer/cardiovascular duet made Mother's death seem imminent again. Bill would leave in mid-August for law school in California. On Labor Day we would take Richard to Boston for the start of college.

I am so scared. So sad. All I do is cry.
My children leave.
My mother dies.
Too much is going from my life.

I had a family dinner to bid the boys good-bye.

Mother's hair in bunches sets my teeth on edge again. Does she think I might forget that she's dependent? Does she feel she needs to *look* the baby part?

Daddy is fat and pink of face and pinker after every gin and tonic.

Alice is terrified. Her sight went blurry early in the week. She saw her doctor who said her blood pressure is too high.

"I'm really scared," she says. "My diabetes doesn't frighten me, but I really do not want a stroke."

My father tries to reassure her. "It's nothing—loss of vision. I've lost my sight a dozen times. Why, just this afternoon I had to go into the bathroom and stay in the dark for forty-five minutes until I could see again."

Terrific.

Mother leaves the table to lie down on the sofa in the den.

"It's hard to sit," she says. "My back and neck . . . and I'm so tired."

My father is preoccupied.

"I'm feeling very strange," he says. "I told Dr. Binnion that I feel as if I'm sitting on top of a volcano."

"What did Dr. Binnion say?"

"He laughed. He said, 'We couldn't do a thing to stop Mount St. Helens, so I don't know what we can do for you.'"

But my father knows.
He shouldn't smoke.

Mother staggers into the kitchen as I'm scraping plates.
"Do you mind if I go now?" she asks. "I'm beat."
Mind to see this walking Mayo Clinic go? Not quite.
"No, I don't mind."
She leans on me and starts to cry.
I hold her close. I rub her back.
Good-bye.

September~October 1980

"I'm starting to have pain, pain," Mother said on September 3.

"Pain" was annoying, but could be stood. "Pain, pain" was suffering.

"And I'm having awful problems with my walking. That little thing in my groin seems to be getting bigger. And my legs buckled three times last week."

The doctor listened as he scanned her eyes. He nodded while he looked down her throat. He attended to her growing list of symptoms with interest every visit.

"Your pressure is fine," he said. "Your heart and lungs sound good."

The neck and underarms were next:

"No lumps?" Mother wondered.

"No, dear, everything's the same."

He tapped her back.

She winced.

"Lie down now, Mildred," he said, lowering her.

"That's my best position." Her eyes were tightly closed.

He felt the breast.

"No lumps?" she asked again.

"No, everything is fine."

He felt the belly . . . then the abdomen . . .

"All is well here, too," he said.

"But not the groin?"

His fingertips were busy. "Maybe not." It looked as if his fingertips were thinking. "You might be right. I think, perhaps, the groin lump *is* a little bigger."

"See? I'm not so dumb. . . ."

"Now lift this leg and kick me hard away, please, honey. Tell me if this hurts. Now let me see you push and tell me if this bothers you at all."

We sat in silence while he wrote, waited patiently as he leafed through his notes. At last, he looked at Mom and shook his head and said, "This is unsatisfactory, Mildred. We must try a different way. You are feeling much too rotten, dear. I think we ought to put you in the hospital. I want to go over you with a fine-tooth comb and find out the exact stage of your metastatic disease. I want to see if any other problem besides cancer is causing all your misery."

"But what about my chemotherapy?" said Mother. "Can I have it this morning?"

"No. I want to take the tests and get results and *then* decide whether or not we ought to change the chemicals you're getting. You can afford to miss a week or two."

And . . . just as pressing . . .

"Can I have a private room?"

Alice took Mom to the hospital while I stayed home and wrote, thus proving things *do* change. And Alice brought her quickly home the moment it was found that someone in Admissions—ignorant of Mother's lineage—had put a partner in her cubicle, thus proving that things always stay entirely the same.

Four-twelve Spruce, a private room, became free the following day. Mother went alone, by cab, because my father wasn't home, my sister was at work, and I was on the track when the admissions office called. When I walked into her room at four o'clock that afternoon I found her nightgowns and her bathrobes on hangers placed the necessary inch apart, the extra towels already filed neatly in the drawer, and the lotions and perfumes properly lined up.

"I did it all myself," said Mother proudly.

She and Dad were arguing:

"If I've told you once," she said, "I've said at least a million times that if you didn't eat so much and if you stopped smoking, you would feel a million percent better."

No matter that *she* smoked three packs a day and regularly overdosed on fats and sugar.

"Oh, for God's sake, let me be," he said.

"But I can't stand to see you so uncomfortable."

"Okay, okay . . . tomorrow I'll begin a diet. In the meantime, where'd you hide the candy?"

"What's going on?" I asked.

"I've been having trouble with my stomach. Something in my abdomen is hurting me," my father said. "Right here. I have a steady pain."

"Why don't you call the doctor?"

"I did. This morning. Thursday I am having X-rays."

"And what about the vascular specialist you said you would see about your legs?" I said.

"I'm seeing him a *week* from Thursday."

"I keep telling him those cigarettes don't help," Mom said.

"They what?" he yelled.

"And will you *please* find out about a hearing aid?" I shouted.

"A what?"

"My birthday is in three weeks," I told my folks. "Do you think you could arrange it so that both of you are moder-

169

ately well that day? I'd consider it a perfect birthday gift if neither one of you was in the hospital on *this* October first."

We laughed. I wasn't kidding.

"You'll be forty-four," Mom said.

"No, Mother. I'll be forty-five." My teeth were clenched. "Why can't you ever get it *right?*"

"Relax," she said. "So I missed a year. Big deal. You're here, aren't you? That's what really matters."

Mother was a different person during that admission. She dropped the Slavic princess act and treated the entire staff—except for doctors who she would *always* see as gods—as peers.

She was genial and full of pep. Her royal needs were still as grand—special pillows, extra towels, a slew of sheets and blankets, vats of cream, and butter and sugar by the pound—but now she hobbled after them herself.

Not only that, but when something ordered didn't come at once, she often shrugged.

Not only that, but *I* didn't have to run a yard of interference.

I don't know why my mother chose that occasion to slam the palace door. Perhaps she thought the doctor's fine-tooth-comb approach contained the promise of a cure. Maybe she was hoping to trade good behavior for remission. Who cared?

I didn't have to do one-tenth as much.

And *everyone* loved Mom.

The nurses could not do enough for her. The orderlies dropped in to give her a quick hug. Maids were spotted cleaning dirt from places maids did not know dirt would go until my mother showed them how *she* worked to rid the world of it.

"Guess who I just met in Ultrasound?" said Mother Thursday afternoon.

"Who?"

"Your father. He was going in to get an upper GI X-ray, just as I was coming back."

The gods reserve such serendipity for very few.

Daddy's films are normal.

"But I know it isn't mental," he kept saying. "I'm in pain."

I kept trying to explain the links between the psyche and the soma and the stress that he was living with, but he refused to listen.

"I'm not nuts," he said. "What I feel is real."

Mother's doctor is "perplexed."

"We see some slight changes in deep tendon reflexes," he said. "And there is some myelopathy from earlier radiation. Some of her misery is from cardiovascular disease, some from chemotherapy, and much of it, I think, is from depression. As far as spread of tumor is concerned—the only thing we definitely see is in the groin. But I want to do more tests."

Why is he perplexed?

That kind of catalog certainly explains her misery to me.

Dr. Daniels, summing up on September 22, announced two changes: Mother's chemotherapy would switch to a low dose of Adriamycin, an antibiotic supposed to be effective against a wide array of tumors, and Vincristine, an agent that interfered with cell division, which would be given intravenously at three-week intervals. Mother would get radiation treatments in the groin, where spread was definite, and in the lower back where it was "highly likely."

The doctor, in addition, was concerned about anemia.

"I want to test and make sure that she isn't losing blood internally," he said. "If nothing is found, we'll give her chemotherapy on Thursday and discharge her Saturday morning. Any questions?"

Yes.

But not about the things I *used* to think I had to know: rads or kinds of chemicals and what they're thought to do, or platelet counts or side effects. Just this:

"If she were *your* mother, Dr. Daniels, would you put her through this?"

And, "What about Sloan-Kettering?"

Plus two that never crossed my lips:

Why her?

When will this be over?

Further X-rays showed two cysts on Daddy's kidneys, which, he was assured, were insignificant—to the doctors, if not to him. But the vascular tests, when matched against those from four years ago, showed the circulation in his legs to be much worse. The next logical step—to see if bypass surgery would help—was an arteriogram.

"I'm scared to death," my father said.

No wonder.

The time pursuant to the shot of dye through his carotid arteries in 1972 was as close to hell as Daddy said he ever came: he had trouble understanding simple words; he couldn't read; his speech was intermittent—words dribbled from his lips. His vision, when not doubled, often blurred. It was months before the side effects of *that* arteriogram wore off.

"But this time things are different," I was saying. "New techniques . . . a better doctor . . ."

"I know," said Dad. "But I'd be lying if I said I wasn't frightened. There is also another problem on my mind. The doctor has me scheduled to go into the hospital on Sunday—the day after Mother's coming home. The timing's terrible. I hate to burden *you* again. . . ."

"But Mother's not much worse than when she went into the hospital three weeks ago," I said. "She managed then, and she'll manage now. You go."

He nodded.

172

"There's another reason why I think I ought to do it. Mother is getting worse. We *know* the cancer has spread. I think that I can do more for her and you and all of us if I am well enough to help."

"Don't worry. We will manage, Daddy. Go."

I meant it. It wasn't fair for him to have to wait to take care of himself until things were easier with Mother. God only knew when that would be. Besides, Mom *had* done all right at home three weeks ago and *splendidly* the first two weeks of her hospitalization. True, the last nine days she had seemed sicker, weaker, worse. . . . But he shouldn't wait. We'd do okay.

I meant it.

But my unconscious must have sensed some subtle tremors. My late September notes contain a daily growing list of things I had to hurry up and do:

Get Mother a new wig.

Beg Leonard Abrams to see Mom and fix her mouth.

Figure out an X-ray schedule so that I can take her for her treatments every day and still have time to write.

Arrange to talk to Daddy's doctor after the arteriogram.

My early-warning system must have sensed impending doom. Whenever I begin arranging things and making lists and making plans compulsively, it means I sense that something bad is coming.

The day we went to take her home, nurses were surrounding Mother, hugging her and saying, "We'll miss you, Mrs. Rubin, but we hope you don't come back." The maid who came to tear apart 412 for a new patient said that it had been a pleasure to "work with such a lovely lady." A tall, young man from escort service told us it had been the highlight of his day to "take the angel for her X-ray treatments this past week."

Mother *was* a different woman during that admission.

173

But Daddy was the same. He reached directly for a five to tip the kid who complimented Mom.

"No, thank you, sir," the escort said. "I really like your wife. I couldn't take a tip for that."

This was the plan:

I would stay at Mother's Saturday to help smooth her transition home while Alice marketed and cooked. On Sunday I would drive Dad to the hospital and Alice would stay with Mom. On Monday I'd pick Mother up at one—thus leaving the morning free for work—head first to X-ray, wait for Mom, and then go up with her to see Pop. We'd do this for the week she had to have additional treatments. Then, depending on my dad's recuperation, we'd make new arrangements.

Saturday we stayed fairly close to schedule. Mother had some nausea and some weakness—"Normal side effects from radiation," the radiologist said—and she had a bit of belly pain, but nothing that a team as organized as we were couldn't handle.

But early Sunday morning, I woke up to the smell of oil and found my water heater steaming, the thermostat at 240° Fahrenheit. Later I would recognize this as a sign the gods were playing table tennis and using us as Ping-Pong balls, but *then* I took it as just another inconvenience, not a portent. So as soon as the repairman reassured us that the house would not blow up, I ran my thirty minutes, showered, dressed, and called my dad to double-check on when I'd pick him up: he wanted to be in his room in time to see the Eagles play.

"Mother spent the night in pain," he said.

That was the second sign I failed to heed.

"Let's bring her out to stay with me," I said. "It would be more comfortable for you and for me if she were here while you're away. Will you try to talk her into it?"

"I already did. She agreed."

We scrap plan A.

Plan B: Alice will bring Mother to my house at two o'clock.

I hurry to the A&P for butter, cream, Saltines, and Nutrament. I race to pick up my father, drop him at the hospital door, pull into the parking lot, grab the ticket, drive in circles until I find an opening on level three, pull the station wagon in, put the car in park, and press the button to put up the window.

A rattling sound announces that the glue that holds the window in place has loosened.

The window falls out of its slot into the framework of the door. I cannot retrieve it, but it is very clear by now that the gaping hole in the car door is omen number three.

My father and I rush to the admissions desk. I take my father's suitcase to his room while he attends to blood tests and a chest X-ray; then I hurry home so I can be on time to greet my guest.

She cannot make it up the steps to Richie's room. She is too weak, in too much pain. I make the sofa in the den into a bed. She cannot sleep. Her nausea is worsening. Compazine and Coca-Cola syrup do not help. The heating pad and aspirin offer no relief. "Have a Darvon . . . take more Valium . . ." I say continually. Her misery so frightens me that I would push a pound of heroin on her if it were mine to give.

She inches toward the bathroom bent and hunched: she's tired, slow. She moans. Only very slowly do the moans turn into whimpers. Only after *hours* does she sleep.

The next five days have this to recommend them: I survived.

(What kind of monster can this be? Who thinks of "I" while Mother writhes in agony and Daddy's lying in the hospi-

175

tal? What kind of creature would describe the time in terms of "me"?)

Behold the week:

Monday: Dr. Daniels puts Mother on a codeine/aspirin plan which the drugstore can't deliver fast enough, so I must hurry to pick up. I make lunch, croon it into her, and watch her throw it up. I drive to the hospital and park in front and swear to God and to the guard that I am only there until I can get Mom in a wheelchair. I run inside and commandeer a chair which I struggle to get through the double doors and outside to the car. I fail to apply the brake and have to stop the chair from rolling with my foot when Mom gets in it. I work my frantic way back to the lobby. "Wait right here," I say. "I'll park the car and be right back."

"Relax," she says to me.

I park the car in the one spot that's left in the entire lot and then race back into the hospital. I grab the chair and push it through the lobby. I bump into three walls and nearly hit a litter. We take the elevator to the basement.

"How long will Mother be?" I ask the nurse.

"No more than twenty minutes."

"Wait for me." I kiss Mom's cheek. She feels too weak to see Dad afterward, so I am going up to visit him in 744 while she is being treated.

"Send him my love and tell him I will talk to him tonight," Mom says.

Dad's roommate is a blond young man who's lying, dressed, upon his bed, his arm around a younger, blonder girl. The television is on. The volume is strangely low. I introduce myself to him in whispers.

"Is my father sleeping?" I inquire.

"I don't know," the young man says. "But he's been pretty sick."

He what?

"The doctors have been in and out all night."

Behind the curtain, chalky Dad, attached to intravenous, sleeps.

I wake him up.

"What's wrong with you?" I say.

"How's Mom?" he wants to know.

"She's fine. But what the hell is wrong with you?"

"My pressure shot up pretty high last night: two-thirty over one twenty-five. They want to bring it down before they do the arteriogram. Now tell me, how is Mom?"

"Terrific. But I have to go. She's tired and I want to get her home."

"I'm tired, too. Tell her I'll talk to her tonight."

I race down to B and up to one and leave Mom in the lobby while I run back for the car and park in front again, tell the guard, get her in, take the wheelchair back, and drive us home so she can vomit.

Dinnertime. She doesn't eat. "Try a milkshake," I implore. She turns her head away. More Compazine.

Dad's arteriogram is scheduled for tomorrow.

I collapse.

I cannot sleep.

Tuesday: She is crouched atop the steps, exhausted from the climb she made to bathe. Her breakfast is long gone. She's weak. I hear her tiny moans. Her belly hurts. Codeine and more Compazine.

Me at Charlie Chaplin speed: the car, the guard, the parking lot. The double doors. The wheelchair running over me. My pop asleep after the arteriogram—flat on his restless back. I wake him up. His speech is thick. "How's Mom?"

"She's fine. She sends her love. She's tired."

"So am I."

Wednesday: The hell with this! I ask for help.

Judy goes with Mom and me to Leonard Abrams who has fit my mother into his busy schedule. He quickly takes impressions, X-rays, and promises a "temporary, comfortable arrangement for your mother by next Wednesday."

177

I thank him and his staff a dozen times.

Judy stays with Mom in Radiation; I grab ten minutes with my dad.

His doctor—De Laurentis—will be in that night to talk about the possibility of surgery. I ask Dad not to forget to tell Dr. De Laurentis to get in touch with me because I can't be there to *hear* what he proposes, since my mother's sick and I must be with her and . . .

My father knows.

"And an early happy birthday," Daddy says as I am kissing him good-bye. "You'll be forty-five tomorrow."

"Thanks, Dad. But I'm forty-five *today.*"

Thursday: Mom's got diarrhea, stomach pain, and unrelenting nausea. My father's groggy, dropping things. I can't decipher what he says the doctor said and I can't reach the doctor. What am I to do?

Through his secretary, I arrange to meet with Dr. De Laurentis late that day to talk about my father's options. What if he must choose between two kinds of surgery? How dare *I* advise him? I am so near hysteria, so full of wishing he or Mom or both of them would die, it's not impossible that I might steer him toward what's easier for *me* instead of good for him.

I must not go alone.

It's come to this: my father needs a better representative. He needs an ombudsman to me!

"Your father's arteries are a mess," the doctor says to me and Daddy's sister Emily. "I have no magic and I can't undo the cardiovascular damage that exists, but I can propose an operation that will help him *walk* more comfortably: an axillofemoral bypass."

He explains and we agree. Surgery will be tomorrow at 8:00 A.M. Dad will spend the weekend in Intensive Care and two weeks in the hospital. He can then look forward to an uneventful recovery at home.

178

It's settled.

Mom won't eat. She tries to sleep. Joel's at a meeting. Alice and I face one another at the dinner table. Both of us are numb.

The telephone rings.

"You won't believe this," Daddy says, "but my surgery is postponed."

"Why?"

"I'm having kidney problems."

No.

"The doctor wants to talk to you. Hold on."

I wait.

"Your father came into the hospital with kidney function tests that weren't great," the resident said. "But for a man of his age, with his conditions, we didn't think them remarkable. Now, however, the kidney function tests are twice as bad and we won't operate until—unless—they're better."

"Is he in any danger?"

"No more than usual."

"Now look . . ."

"Don't worry," said the resident. "I'm sure it isn't serious."

Oh, no.

Mother's going home tomorrow.

"I can't continue to impose on you and Joel," she insists between her thanks and moans. "You've both been wonderful, but my sisters will take care of me for part of the weekend and Alice will be there. On Monday Phyllis will be in and she will stay the week. Maybe once the radiation is done I'll be feeling better."

I ask Debbie to help me do tomorrow's moving.

Friday: Debbie comes to the hospital with Mom and me. While they descend to B, I visit Dad who's waiting for the latest kidney tests. He doesn't ask for Mother until I leave.

Deb and I race through the now-familiar going-home-from-hospital routine and then we switch Mom to a rented wheelchair, push her through the lobby of her apartment house, and take her to her place, where she crawls into bed and tries to sleep. Deb and I unpack the food that she had picked up at the market, make menus for next week, and speak of better ways to age. Aunt Ethel arrives, then Yetta. Debbie leaves. I go home and make myself a giant drink, write some notes, take the calls, and thank the family and friends for their attention. I make a date for eight o'clock tomorrow night to have a ten-course Szechwan banquet in honor of my birthday.

I survived. I got us through the week. Mother got her radiation, Daddy got good care, and I didn't use the pressure and the tension and my almost total lack of sleep as an excuse to pick on Alice.
Sometimes I even laughed.
This time I did it right.

Survive?
I triumphed!

My father spent the weekend in the hospital pitying my mother—"She must feel so horribly alone"—and waiting for his kidneys to improve. Mother grew more wretched and much weaker. My sister reached new heights: she braved the fear she must have felt and stayed with Mother overnight and heard her moan and watched her retch and didn't call me *once* for reassurance.

What comfort that my sister can be counted on to share the load, I wrote. *Who says that things don't change?*
She is an angel.

"Get the hell out of my house!"
I screamed so hard that something popped in my ear.
"Son of a bitch!" I shook. "Get out of here and don't you ever threaten me again."

"I wasn't threatening," yelled Alice. "But I can't go there anymore. . . . It's killing me. She's like a child—whining all the time—she's so sick. . . . It's horrible."

"Don't tell me that you can't go there. You can't abandon everything to *me!*"

"It's hard for me, too, you know," she said. "You're not the only one in this."

Who cared about how hard it was for *her?* She didn't have to do one-ninetieth of what was mine. She had to help *me* through this nightmare or get out.

"Get out of here," I said. "And don't you ever tell me that you can't go there again."

"You're a maniac," she screamed. "How come you're always nice to everyone but me?"

I should have understood that she was scared. I should have just accepted nonjudgmentally the way she felt, and known that once she had unloaded she would feel much better and be back. I should have patted her and reassured her and told her how I needed her strength—not someone *else* I had to help.

But whoever knows from "shoulds" when terror strikes?

I screamed.

Sure she was malingering. I went to Mother's place on Monday morning, hell-bent on seeing to it that she got her body out of bed.

"Come on. I've made a milkshake," I cajoled. "And Phyllis has some tuna fish. They're in the kitchen. Lean on me. We'll walk in there."

"I don't think I can make it."

"Come on, Mother." I was firm. "You're getting up! Right now! It isn't good for you to lie in bed like this. You'll end up with pneumonia."

I draped myself on top of her and wrapped her arms around my neck and held her back.

"That hurts."

"Come on."

I pulled her up.

She fell out of my arms onto the floor.

At two o'clock my father shows. "Aunt Bea drove me home," he says. "The doctor discharged me and said that if I lose twenty-five pounds and stop smoking it will do me more good than any bypass surgery."

"See?" my mother says. "I'm not so dumb."

"Is Mother terminal?" I asked Dr. Daniels the following morning.

"Definitely not."

"Then something is very wrong," I said and ran through all her symptoms: nausea; diarrhea; pain in belly and back; lack of appetite; overwhelming weakness.

"You're absolutely right," he said. "Something's very wrong. I want her readmitted to the hospital."

"Mother will want a private room if you can see to it."

"I'll see what is available, but I'm not waiting if one isn't free. We'll take whatever they have. Get back to me in fifteen minutes."

Only one bed in the hospital was left. It was in a room for two.

"I'm waiting until they have a private room," my mother moaned. "And that is *definite*."

She really meant it: better dead than semiprivate!

"Oh no, Mom. Not this time. You're much too sick. This time you have no choice."

I mobilized a medical safari: Dad and Phyllis packed Mom's things, sat her in a wheelchair, and took her to the lobby, where the doorman helped my father put Mom in the car that Joel waited in to take her to the hospital, where I would meet her and ease her through Admissions.

But none of my deployment skills could ease her misery.

We waited in the hall while Mother's room was being readied. She made four bathroom trips in forty minutes. She sighed in pain and tried to fight off nausea. In between laments she sent me off to scout for extra towels, extra sheets, and blankets.

"Do me a favor," Mother must have said a dozen times.

"Get me an extra pillow . . . call housekeeping . . . tell them not to make it hard. . . . Another favor, please, if you don't mind. Ask them at the nurses' station for extra body lotion, extra mouthwash, and more tissues."

When not directing me, she ordered Dad around.

"Do me a favor, Sy. Get me a cup of water and see that the television set's connected."

What had happened to the sweet and ordinary lady she had been two weeks ago? What had put her back on the road between the court at Moscow and the palace at St. Petersburg again? I liked her more as commonfolk. Such a spoiled brat, I thought. So horribly demanding.

And yet . . . as sick and weak as Mother was she asked Nurse L. about her mother who, two weeks ago, was very sick. She reminded me to bring some clothes that Richie had outgrown for the maid's teen-aged grandson.

But still she could not stand the semiprivateness of things.

"Where's my roommate?" Mother whispered as I was helping her undress.

"Who knows? Maybe she's in X-ray."

"What do I do if she doesn't want to watch the same programs that I do?"

"You compromise," I said.

She looked at me as if I needed a lobotomy.

"What if she's not clean?"

"Good Christ!" I cried. "You're acting crazy, Mother. Stop it! I know it's hard for you, but my God, stop acting like a baby. You are *sick*. You're in a *hospital*. It's not a spa. I know you don't believe it, but a semiprivate room is not the worst thing in the world."

She wore a punished little girl look.

"It's not?"

I didn't laugh.

183

"Daddy's downstairs in Admissions now, telling them as soon as there's an empty private room, we want it. In the meantime, can't you try to make the best of things?"

"I'll try," she said.

She cried.

I could have kicked myself. How could I be impatient with so sick and sad a lady? I should have understood that she was scared. I should have just accepted nonjudgmentally the way she felt, and known that once she had unloaded she would feel much better. I should have patted her and reassured and . . . I should have been somebody else.

The roommate—Theresa—a heavy, eighty-nine-year-old white-haired woman, seemed nice enough, but who could know? She didn't speak a word of English. A plus was that she didn't bother Mother with a lot of conversation. A minus, though, was all the noisy meetings with the people on the staff who didn't understand Italian.

I was also praying for a private room.

Theresa's single visitor—a sullen niece who came each day at four o'clock—was walking proof of just how ugly duty done unlovingly could be.

The niece's body, always yardstick stiff, was always distant from her aunt. Her narrow lips were set in an ominous straight line. She rarely spoke and when she did her words were wrapped in quick, impatient packages one didn't need to know Italian to interpret.

Not once did I see her touch Theresa.

Never did I see her smile.

What had Aunt Theresa's life been like to lead to this hostility? I wondered.

And what on earth could I do not to end up like her?

Spare me, please, the curse of being cared for by someone who doesn't care for me at all.

I swear to God I'll never yell at Mom again.

A single room became available on Friday morning.

"Thank you, God, oh, thank you," Mother murmured as I packed.

At noon she moved to 751, the place where she would spend the next nine weeks in *private* misery.

October–December 1980

More than two years after the beginning of my parents' serious decline, my life had come full circle: one parent in the hospital again; the other not yet hospitalized, but ailing.

Mother had incontinence induced from radiation, which the doctors hoped that cortisone enemas would cure. She had a low white count, from chemotherapy, which everybody thought would surely rise. She had headaches, nausea, and an overwhelming misery that supported the cliché that the cure is often worse than the disease.

But there were other symptoms during the next nine weeks that supported the conclusion that disease—alone—would do.

She had tremors, memory lapses. A little stroke was diagnosed—"an ischemic episode." She lost her appetite. Her weight, when she could make it to the scale, was eighty-two; they gave her intravenous feedings. She coughed and got a fever and her lungs filled up. "Pneumonia," we were told, "but a very mild case." Her blood pressure roller-coastered so dramatically that Dr. Daniels said that "Dr. Cook went to his books to see if he can figure out what's going on."

She had a spinal tap.

"We suspect some tumor in the fluid, but can't be absolutely sure without some tests that I'm not certain we should make because they're so invasive."

She had two transfusions.

My father smoked too much and nibbled sweets as he sat faithfully beside my mother's bed throughout the next nine weeks. His sleep was fitful; he was constantly fatigued. The strain of coming to the hospital each day, compounded with the worry and confusion and the maddening uncertainty, showed in his face: his coloring turned gray; his eyes were often red; his forehead vein throbbed constantly.

I was in my panic mode again, obsessed with the old questions: How could I attend to him, take care of her, and keep myself intact? How could I stand the guilt again? The anger? The worry and the pain?

How could I stand to be the same old self?

More than two years later we had come full circle.

She doesn't know the Phillies won last night—a dire sign. She sleeps. I sit by her bed and think that I have brought some peace to her, some ease. I think we have settled things.

"Do me a favor, please," she murmurs. "Please . . . if you don't mind . . ."

Anything.

"Rub my legs and back with cocoa butter for a little while."

I smooth the bony body lovingly.

"It feels so good."

I rub and knead and say how much I love her and how glad I am that I can give her comfort.

"You do," she says. "You have. You ought to be a nurse's aide."

"A nurse's aide?" I scream. "Mother! Is that really all you want for me?"

I lecture her on expectations and the awful injustice of a society that encourages women to be aides, not doctors.

She shrugs. "What do you want from me?" she says. "I'm not thinking much about the ERA these days."

"But what *are* you thinking of?" I ask.

She turns her tired body slowly over and she looks at me, again, as if I need brain surgery.

We laugh.

But I'm not kidding.

I want to know, the way I did two years ago. I want to hear from Mother's lips exactly what she thinks and how she feels about what's happening to her. I want to know it all again. I want to have her talk to me and walk me through each piece of her experience. It is as if—through her—I want to practice patienthood. It is as if I wish she would provide me with a dry run for my dying.

I also want her suffering to *mean* something.

I cannot stand the thought that Mother's torment is completely random.

But she will not cooperate. She was *never* given to a lot of talk about her inner state. Unfamiliar with the sharing fad, dumb to verbal road maps of emotion that declare where one is "coming from," my mother cannot do a psychic strip. She sulks or cries or bitches when she's "nervous" or "depressed"—but privately. When I ask what lies behind her misery, she always says she cannot say. She says she doesn't know. I always have to guess.

And if I knew?

And if she said?

What would either of us have really gained?

Only very slowly during the following nine weeks did it begin to dawn on me that the sicker Mother got, the less relevant *talk* was to what was happening. I came to see that even if she spoke nonstop, nothing would be gained. Words couldn't make her suffering make sense to me, nor could they do a thing to ease *her* anguish.

Long days at the hospital again.
"I was there five hours yesterday and I swear she didn't say a word," my father says.
He's tired. Hospital vigils take their toll.
"I think he's depressed," my sister says. "He's coming here for dinner tonight, but I'm not sure that I'm the one to cheer him up."
He eats the fudge I bring for the floor nurses and finishes what's left on Mother's tray. He's gaining weight and smoking more than ever.

She doesn't watch the Phillies play.
"What time is it?" she wants to know.
"Three-thirty."
"Is that all? It goes so damned slowly. . . ."
Time.
The lady in the room next door is dying. The family goes in and out in tears. Each time I pass I peek at the private-duty nurses and somebody I assume is the dying lady's almost-always-crying daughter.
Soon I will be you, I think.
Poor thing, to be without your mother.
Time.
The waits until I reach the doctor on the phone. Eternities on hold until Reception connects the nurse, the nurse connects the doctor, and finally Dr. Daniels talks to me.
He's always full of hope, which never fits the weak and wretched mother that I see.
"I'm sending her for physical therapy to try to help her walking. I am confident your mother will improve," he says.
He's crazy.

189

He is right.

She wears ribbons around the hideous bunches one surprising afternoon, lipstick the next day, rouge the day after, and then she starts the questions that always drive me crazy:

"Are you warm enough? Do you know that you should wash that in cold water? Where did you park? You won't take the expressway home? Have you spoken to the boys since Sunday night?"

She's interested in things outside herself again. She wants to know how Debbie's kids are doing. She asks for Ina's boys. She wants to hear once more the tale of Judy's poker-playing escapades and begs for more about Maxine and Arthur's party.

She's too alive, she can't be dying.

The doctor must be right.

No, she has belly pain again. Her back hurts so much that she can barely turn. She has headaches, tremors. She has another tiny stroke.

Alice, Dad, and I come together in the hallway or the waiting room and whisper: What does the doctor think will happen next? What did he say *today?* What will we do if it goes on like this? What if she can't walk? If she's in pain? How can we make her comfortable? How can we cope? How long will this go on?

The three of us were perplexed constantly. And, although we never got a single, satisfactory answer, we never stopped the endless questions, would not give up the constant effort to make sense of what we knew would always be entirely beyond our ken.

The three of us spent hours trying to decipher what insurance policies would pay. "Understanding Medicare" and "What Phoenix Mutual Will Do" became our bedtime reading. It felt unseemly to be worried about money while Mother was so sick; concerns about what things cost seemed hideously wrong. Yet we couldn't order private nurses if insurance didn't cover it. We had to estimate the cost of having Phyllis every day if Mother ever managed to get home.

While it was strange to speak of money matters, money, more than ever, seemed to matter.

The three of us were newly gentle to each other:

"Don't worry, Daddy, you are not alone in this. . . ."

"You kids have been terrific. . . ."

"Why don't you take the weekend off? I'll come and stay both days."

We were closer, more dependent on each other; we were more scared than ever.

We huddled tight like fingers in a mitten.

She's perkier; she's worse. She's better; bad again.
She's coming home.
She's not.
She has pneumonia.

Time.

"How much?" I ask a doctor who is covering for Daniels on the weekend after Mother gets pneumonia. "How much time do you think Mother has?"

He doesn't want to be pinned down.

"How much?"

I am so tired of her suffering, so sick of sitting in the chair next to her bed watching, waiting, hating running back and forth, fearing what the stress is doing to my dad.

I would gladly trade a limb to have a *limit* on this trial.

"How long?"

He shrugs.

"Do you think it will be years . . . or months . . . or weeks?" I won't let up.

"Well . . . if it goes on like this . . . if she continues weakening . . . not eating . . . then I would say it could be fairly soon."

"How soon?" I push.

"It could be weeks," he says reluctantly.

Weeks.

"Weeks" cuts through me like a knife.

I cry.

He can't be telling me that there will shortly be a world without my mother in it. I do not want my mother dead. I want her *here*. I want her here to criticize, to rage against, resent. I love her, yes—but that's not the only reason I don't want her to die.

I am a child.

I simply want my mother.

But there is another side to "weeks"—a soothing side. It is the boundary that I've been praying for; its promise of a limit makes me feel alive. I can stand *anything* for weeks. I can postpone my other living, look after Mother constantly, see to my father's needs, be a loving pal to Alice, organize a proper funeral, tell the boys to make sure that their suits are pressed and shoes are shined. . . .

"Weeks" is somehow comforting.

But Mother doesn't die.

She fades one day, the next she's better and there's nothing I can plan on except spending my days in waiting, running back and forth, and worrying.

My days.

Remember this, you selfish bitch. While you are trying to make sure you get enough, your mother is in hell.

You juggle.

Mother struggles for her life.

I spin. I reel myself back in.

Is this my destiny? To be the Queen of Yo-Yos?

There is a storm in me. My arms and neck and middle must explode. I cannot stand it anymore. It's more than two years later and it's still the same old thing: resentment, rage, and love.

The goddamned guilt.

The nine-week hospital stay is like a replay of the more than two past years: The peace I've made turns into war when she is vague. I find myself enraged about the drink she swears she ordered.

"You didn't write it down," I say. I push the menu toward her. "Here's the proof. You didn't circle 'Coke.' "

"I did."

"But, Mother, look."

"Oh, please, leave me alone."

"Why won't you just admit? . . ."

"What do you want from me?"

I do not say.

We fight.

I despise her.

I swear I'll stay away.

Please let her die.

I've come full vicious circle.

We both apologize.

We cry.

She sleeps.

She sobs.

"This is so hard. . . . I feel so horrible for what I'm doing to the three of you."

I wrap my arms around her, draw her head and chest to me. Her body droops. I kiss her head. I rub her neck. I stroke her back. She is all bone. All Buchenwald.

I weep.

"I love you very much," I say.

Four hours afterward I'm at a clambake, drinking wine and laughing, devouring succulent crabs and mussels. I dance. After a Virginia reel, Mary Catherine stops to chat.

"How's your mother doing?" she inquires.

"Not so good," I say.

"And you?" she asks. "How are *you* holding up?"

What shall I say? Shall I—between the sips and smiles—run on about how difficult things are for *me?*

I have the grace not to complain. But still, I must indulge myself in *some* self-conscious statement:

"I'm okay, I guess. But I'm ashamed that I am having so much fun while Mother's lying—maybe dying—in the hospital. I feel like I'm half monster."

"Don't be so hard on yourself," she says. "It's normal. Don't forget, you're only human."

That seems to be a big part of the problem.

Miriam is full of sympathy each time I call to let her know how Mother is.

"Send her my love and tell her I will come to see her if and when she wants me."

"What can *I* do?" I say.

"Make your peace. Just do the things you can't do when she isn't here."

Terrific, just what I need.

Philosophy.

Plop me in a monastery in Tibet and maybe after forty years I'll learn to live entirely aware and always in the present. But in *my* skin, in Philadelphia, I don't do well perched on a brink. I never get enough said or enough done and every time I try I drive myself and everyone around me nearly crazy.

Give me things to *do*. Give me motions that have *meanings*. I need solids now. Not mush. Do not tell me how to bury ghosts.

Ghosts do not die.

Nor does my mom.

She's coming home on Tuesday.

No.

There might be tumor in the spinal fluid.
She is better.
No.
She's not.

"If you ever get to Israel again, you'll see a lot of trees there planted in my name," she said one day when she was not in too much pain to talk.

"How come?" I asked.

"People are planting trees these days instead of sending flowers to the hospital. Or perfume."

"Does it please you, Mom?"

"Not really. I'd rather have a bottle of Norell."

Sick or well—she is still Mildred.

Miriam suggested that I talk to Dr. Daniels about getting Mother in the hospice program.

"I'm sure Dr. Daniels has avoided recommending hospice to your mother for fear she'd think she would be dead within a month," said Miriam. "But tell him that I think it's time. You *all* can use their help. Besides, I know the people in the program and they're very good."

I knew them, too.

I used to think I would be one of them.

"Did the hostage people get in touch with you?" said Mother. "They said they wanted to set up a family meeting."

"You mean *hospice*, Mother. The *hostages* are in Iran."

"Oh, please," she flicked off my correction. "Hostage . . . hospice . . . what the hell's the difference in the end?"

It came as no surprise that someone from the hospice team would visit Mother daily in the hospital and listen. Listening, I'd learned ten months ago, was a big part of their package. Nor was it unexpected that their emphasis on

195

management of symptoms and prevention and control of pain would give Mom another comfort monitor. After all, the hospice staff was *there* to make things easier for the gravely ill.

This sign—taped to Mother's bathroom mirror on December 3—typified their thinking, I decided:

PLEASE MIX SALINE SOLUTION WITH MOUTHWASH TO EASE SORENESS OF MRS. RUBIN'S GUMS.

SUGGESTED BY THE HOSPICE DEPT.

It was concrete and very kind.

But what converted me and finally turned me into a hospice proselytizer was what they did for *family*.

For me.

There is a blurry quality of life for families of the long-term very ill—a lack of edge, a sense of moving in molasses through distorted time. The lack of crispness and the little you can do to alter things lead to strange fantasies; you pray for boundaries, for ends. Which must be why the hospice seemed a dream come nearly true: they walked into our limbo and came up with some *specifics*.

It seemed, to me, to be a miracle.

In our meeting with the hospice psychiatrist and hospice social worker, we made it clear we didn't wish to share our feelings and frustrations anymore. What was the point? Although we certainly had not run out of howls, we knew too well how futile howls could be.

Ginette, the social worker/nurse who would become *our* ombudsman, took one good look and saw we needed shoring up and that is what she did: she started calling many of our questions in to Dr. Daniels, thus sparing us some waiting time. She got back to us promptly. She didn't rush, and gave us time for follow-up questions.

Day after ever-changing day she tried to find an answer that would hold, tried to straighten out each morning's new confusion. Not that she ever got a firmer grasp than we: truth eludes the hospice people, too. But someone else was trying to assess the situation. Not just me.

196

And somebody, besides me, was representing *us*.

When, in mid-December, it looked as if my tough old mother would recover for what seemed to be the seven hundredth time—and would be coming home—Ginette helped us figure out what Mom would need and what would help the three of us.

She talked about equipment. We agreed that Mother ought to have a wheelchair and a walker.

"I'll see that they're delivered to your place," she said to my dad.

Were we clear about the medications?

"I'll get a list of everything she takes from Dr. Daniels. I'll have him write prescriptions so if you need more drugs there won't be any hassle."

Medical checks on Mom?

"A visiting nurse will see her once a week. Someone from the hospice team—usually Joanne or I—will make regular home visits. We'll also arrange for blood tests if the doctor thinks she needs them."

How to keep in touch?

"We're on twenty-four-hour call if you have any questions. Or if you're worried about something. Or if you simply want to speak to someone."

What is the best way to get Mother home?

"I'll have an ambulance here at ten o'clock on Tuesday."

Perhaps they seem like trivial things—some phone calls and some simple arrangements. But to us—to *me* especially—it was a blessing to have someone else in charge.

Hospice helped us graciously.

Hospice was a godsend.

And *still* we were in hell.

Home Mother came to Phyllis every day; me marketing, Alice and I preparing meals and alternating nights to serve; Daddy pitching in but needing rest and extra nitroglycerine when his heart rebelled, which it did very often.

We hired a nurse from two to ten at night.

My mother waxed; she waned.

We waited once again for Dr. Daniels. The wonder was that he never once gave up on Mother—not even when she said she was through.

He always knew she didn't mean it.

"Think about it, Mildred dear," he said to her request to stop all medication. "I will do it if you like, but I think you're just depressed. I believe you really want to live and if you *do* you know that I will fight for you as long as I am able and as long as you can indicate that you want me to."

He *knew* she wanted to continue.

And she does.

And *still* it is a hell.

Bill and Rich are home from school at Christmas. They visit Mother faithfully and give her a little bit of life, a little bit of holiday.

"They give me so much joy, I cry from pleasure," Mother says.

I am proud because my children do not look upon their visits to their grandmother as a chore.

"We love her, Mom," they say. "Stop thanking us so much. It's no big deal."

As I am more than willing to point out to him at not infrequent intervals, Joel is imperfect as a person and deficient as a husband a hundred times a week. But here, these past two years, where big-league games are being played, he's been my Willie Mays.

He's my Ali.

He's been accepting and supportive and not once from him has come the ugly "that's enough."

He's been, without a doubt, the very greatest.

My friends are loyal, loving sympathizers. The family is here, and Phyllis who keeps telling me, "I'll never leave your mother." We have nurses, Dr. Daniels, Dr. Cook, consultants if we want them, Miriam, the hospice team . . .

And it remains a hell.

And if it is a hell for me, what must it be for her?

We're more confused than ever and we wonder what will happen when the family machine runs down and, finally, out of energy—out of what are euphemistically referred to as resources.

What will we do?

Back and forth to the apartment now, tired all the time again. Somebody mentioned NURSING HOME last night.

God forbid a million times.

Daddy's holding Mother's hand. "I love you," he is telling her, "and I'm glad you're here. Who cares if you're confined to bed? You're part of me. I love you."

The tenderness—in front of me—is new.

My sister says that I should count on her for all the meals next week. I will. And she'll come through.

My father isn't sleeping well. He has to give Mom pills at midnight and at 6:00 A.M. which means his rest is interrupted, which isn't good for his conditions. His face turned red the other night when he was filling up the dishwasher. I wonder what will happen when it hits. . . . What will I do?

I know.

I'll hate it and I'll bitch and moan and cry.

And cope.

And Alice, too.

Mother waxes; Mother wanes.

I wish she would get better.

I wish to hell she'd die.

"I only hope your daughters-in-law are a tenth as good to you as you have been to me," said Mother yesterday.

"What about my sons?" I said.

She laughed. "Sons don't do like daughters. And most daughters aren't half as good as you."

"But, Mom, my sons are good."

"God forbid a million times," she said, "that you should ever have to count on sons, or daughters-in-law, or anyone. . . ."

She's right.

God forbid a million times.

I, too, would rather *die* than be a burden. . . .

Afterword

Mother doesn't like to hear us call it morphine.

"Just say it's *medicine,*" she says about the cherry-colored liquid which my father pours each evening into plastic four-ounce cups for her to take at four-hour intervals the following day.

"Please. Call it medicine. I don't like the other word."

She ought to move her body more. Bed sores are threatening to form. But moving eats up energy. And hurts.

"She isn't terminal," Dr. Daniels told me recently. "There isn't any sign a vital organ is involved. She's strong. I wouldn't be surprised if we are here a year from now, talking about Mother."

Not me, I think.

Not here.

I will be dead—tension and exhaustion will have finished me. Or I will have killed her.

One day I will see her weep too much. I will finally believe her when she says she wants to die.

I have to get away.

We proceed.

Tired, kind, impatient, and afraid.

Sometimes I think suffering has made us tough, and that is what explains the little bit of family strength that's left.

Sometimes I think that this ordeal has tempered me. I think I am less bossy than I was when it began. I think I've learned about the fleetingness of things and so I tell my dear ones often that I love them, and try to note the beauty in the everyday.

Sometimes I think I'm smarter than I was three years ago. I think I know much more about what counts and how to live. I value simple, loving, honest relationships more than ever, and I admire people who are are disciplined and self-controlled . . . and yet . . .

I *still* can be abrupt with Mother, *still* can wish my father different, *still* can sometimes sit in icy judgment of my sister. I still can sulk and nag my kids and rage and curse the fool who cuts in front of me on the expressway.

I am still me.

Except that I forgive myself a little bit more often than before.

Sometimes I think the only change has been a small gain in self-knowledge: I have been a good daughter, and I can be counted on.

Sometimes that seems like quite a lot.

Mildred Rubin died November 17, 1981.